James Newton Poling
Christie Cozad Neuger
Editors

Charles Pringle

Men's Work
in Preventing Violence
Against Women

Men's Work in Preventing Violence Against Women has been co-published simultaneously as *Journal of Religion & Abuse,* Volume 4, Number 3 2002.

Pre-publication
REVIEWS,
COMMENTARIES,
EVALUATIONS . . .

" **A** POWERFUL, PRACTICAL BOOK. . . . Clearly lays out various aspects of men's violence and specific ways that faith communities can begin to address this epidemic in our society. Pastoral leaders need to read this book and recommend it to men's groups. Men in our faith communities need to read and discuss this book to begin the important work of reflecting on the way they were raised, on scripture that has been used to justify male control, and on ways that our faith communities need to change. SEMINARY STUDENTS NEED TO READ THIS BOOK before assuming ministerial leadership."

Bill Ratliff, PhD
Professor of Pastoral Care and Counseling
Earlham School of Religion

"Curious about the cultural and religious narratives that support violence against women? Want to understand why males have difficulty recognizing females as 'other' and their need to control women? Would you like to identify religious messages that contribute to male violence, and also those that can bring change? Want to assess how premarital counsel and wedding rituals speak to marital violence? Interested in increasing male empathy toward female victims and enabling the church to do a more creative job in changing patterns of violence toward women? More personally, are you interested in confronting, confessing, and changing your own conscious and unconscious narratives concerning attitudes and behaviors that cause or allow violence toward women? THEN YOU HAVE COME TO THE RIGHT BOOK!"

Andrew D. Lester, PhD
Professor of Pastoral Theology
and Pastoral Counseling
Brite Divinity School
Texas Christian University

"THIS IS A WELCOME BOOK. As a teacher of pastoral theology and pastoral care, I will use it not only because it presents concrete strategies and helpful resources for ending violence against women from a variety of theological and cultural perspectives, but also because it models how to confront destructive power relations between social groups."

Kathleen D. Billman, PhD
Professor of Pastoral Theology
and Dean of Academic Affairs
Lutheran School of Theology at Chicago

"A VALUABLE RESOURCE. . . . Demonstrates ways religious sources in Jewish and Christian traditions reject violence against women. . . . Offers motivation and guidance for men who are willing to assume accountability. . . . Accessible and substantive, this is a volume for religious leaders and seminary classrooms as well as persons of faith who engage these issues with those whose lives are affected by violence."

Nancy J. Ramsey, PhD
Harrison Ray Anderson
Professor of Pastoral Theology
Louisville Presbyterian Theological Seminary

Men's Work
in Preventing Violence
Against Women

Men's Work in Preventing Violence Against Women has been co-published simultaneously as *Journal of Religion & Abuse,* Volume 4, Number 3 2002.

The *Journal of Religion & Abuse* Monographic "Separates"

Below is a list of "separates," which in serials librarianship means a special issue simultaneously published as a special journal issue or double-issue *and* as a "separate" hardbound monograph. (This is a format which we also call a "DocuSerial.")

."Separates" are published because specialized libraries or professionals may wish to purchase a specific thematic issue by itself in a format which can be separately cataloged and shelved, as opposed to purchasing the journal on an on-going basis. Faculty members may also more easily consider a "separate" for classroom adoption.

"Separates" are carefully classified separately with the major book jobbers so that the journal tie-in can be noted on new book order slips to avoid duplicate purchasing.

You may wish to visit Haworth's Website at . . .

http://www.HaworthPress.com

. . . to search our online catalog for complete tables of contents of these separates and related publications.

You may also call 1-800-HAWORTH (outside US/Canada: 607-722-5857), or Fax 1-800-895-0582 (outside US/Canada: 607-771-0012), or e-mail at:

docdelivery@haworthpress.com

Men's Work in Preventing Violence Against Women, edited by James Newton Poling, PhD, and Christie Cozad Neuger (Vol. 4, No. 3, 2002). *Examines the potential for men/women partnerships to work toward an end to domestic violence and sexual abuse*

Remembering Conquest: Feminist/Womanist Perspectives on Religion, Colonization, and Sexual Violence, edited by Nantawan Boonprasat Lewis, BDiv, ThM, PhD, and Marie M. Fortune, MDiv, DHLit (Vol. 1, No. 2, 1999). *Addresses the issue of sexual violence against Native American, African American, Filipino, and Thai women from feminist/womanist theological perspectives and advocates for change in how some religious groups interpret women.*

Men's Work
in PreventingViolence
Against Women

James Newton Poling, PhD
Christie Cozad Neuger, PhD
Editors

Men's Work in Preventing Violence Against Women has been
co-published simultaneously as *Journal of Religion & Abuse,* Volume 4, Number 3 2002.

The Haworth Pastoral Press
An Imprint of
The Haworth Press, Inc.
New York • London

Published by

The Haworth Pastoral Press, 10 Alice Street, Binghamton, NY 13904-1580 USA

The Haworth Pastoral Press is an imprint of The Haworth Press, Inc., 10 Alice Street, Binghamton, NY 13904-1580 USA.

Men's Work in Preventing Violence Against Women has been co-published simultaneously as *Journal of Religion & Abuse*, Volume 4, Number 3 2002.

Cover design by Marylouise E. Doyle.

Library of Congress Cataloging-in-Publication Data

Men's work in preventing violence against women / James Newton Poling and Christie Cozad Neuger, editors.
     p. cm.
     Simultaneously published as Journal of Religion & Abuse, volume 4, number 3, 2002.
     Includes bibliographical references and index.
     ISBN 0-7890-2171-4 (case : alk. paper)–ISBN 0-7890-2172-2 (pbk: alk paper)
     1. Family violence–Prevention. 2. Family violence–Religios aspects. 3. Women–Crimes against–Prevention 4. Sexual abuse victims–Pastoral counseling of. 5. Victims of family violence–Pastoral counseling of. I. Poling, James Newton. II. Neuger, Christie Cozad. III. Journal of religion & abuse.

HV6626.M46 2003
362.82'92–dc21
                                       · 2003006697

Indexing, Abstracting & Website/Internet Coverage

This section provides you with a list of major indexing & abstracting services. That is to say, each service began covering this periodical during the year noted in the right column. Most Websites which are listed below have indicated that they will either post, disseminate, compile, archive, cite or alert their own Website users with research-based content from this work. (This list is as current as the copyright date of this publication.)

(continued)

Special Bibliographic Notes related to special journal issues (separates) and indexing/abstracting:

- indexing/abstracting services in this list will also cover material in any "separate" that is co-published simultaneously with Haworth's special thematic journal issue or DocuSerial. Indexing/abstracting usually covers material at the article/chapter level.
- monographic co-editions are intended for either non-subscribers or libraries which intend to purchase a second copy for their circulating collections.
- monographic co-editions are reported to all jobbers/wholesalers/approval plans. The source journal is listed as the "series" to assist the prevention of duplicate purchasing in the same manner utilized for books-in-series.
- to facilitate user/access services all indexing/abstracting services are encouraged to utilize the co-indexing entry note indicated at the bottom of the first page of each article/chapter/contribution.
- this is intended to assist a library user of any reference tool (whether print, electronic, online, or CD-ROM) to locate the monographic version if the library has purchased this version but not a subscription to the source journal.

Men's Work in Preventing Violence Against Women

CONTENTS

ABOUT THE EDITORS

James Newton Poling, PhD, is a seminary professor, a Presbyterian minister, and a pastoral psychotherapist. He has worked on issues of domestic violence since 1985 and has written several books on religious issues of abuse, including *The Abuse of Power: A Theological Problem* and *Balm for Gilead: Pastoral Care of African American Families Experiencing Abuse*.

Christie Cozad Neuger, PhD, has served as a pastor, chaplain, pastoral counselor, and professor. An ordained United Methodist elder, she received her Master of Divinity from United Theological Seminary of the Twin Cities and her PhD from Claremont School of Theology, where she received the President's Award for Academic Excellence. Dr. Neuger is a Diplomate in the American Association of Pastoral Counselors and Chair of the Society for Pastoral Theology. Besides numerous articles and chapters, Dr. Neuger is the author of *Counseling Women: A Narrative Pastoral Approach*, editor of *The Arts of Ministry: Feminist-Womanist Approaches*, and co-editor of *The Care of Men*.

About the Contributors

Larry Graham is Professor of Pastoral Theology and Care at Iliff School of Theology in Denver, Colorado. He is ordained in the United Church of Christ and a Diplomate in the American Association of Pastoral Counselors. He has written two books, *Care of Persons, Care of Worlds*, and *Discovering Images of God.*

Christopher Grundy is an ordained United Church of Christ minister, a former pastor, who is currently a PhD student in liturgical studies at Garrett-Evangelical Theological Seminary.

Paul Kivel is a trainer, activist, and writer. He was a cofounder of the Oakland Men's Project and of Gvarim: Bay Area Jewish Men Against Violence and is the author of several books including *Men's Work: How to Stop the Violence that Tears Our Lives Apart,* and *Uprooting Racism: How White People Can Work for Racial Justice.*

David Livingston is Assistant Professor of Religious Studies, Mercyhurst College, Erie, PA, and is the author of *Healing Violent Men: A Model for Christian Communities.*

Al Miles works for Pacific Health Ministry as Coordinator of the hospital ministry for Pacific Health Ministry at The Queen's Medical Center, Honolulu, Hawaii. He is author of *Domestic Violence: What Every Pastor Should Know*, and *Violence in Families: What Every Christian Needs to Know.*

Hahnshik Min is pastor of the LaMoine River Parish of the United Methodist Chruch and Macomb Korean Fellowship, and lives in Blandinsville, Illinois.

Ted Stoneeberg is Professor of Pastoral Care and Counseling, Anderson School of Theology, Anderson, Indiana, an ordained minister in the Evangelical Lutheran Church in America, and author of numerous articles including "How Should We Conceive the Tasks of Men in Families?" in The Family Handbook.

Richard Wallace teaches pastoral care and counseling at Luther Seminary in St. Paul, MN. He is the editor for the *Journal of Ministry in Addiction and Recovery*. He continues to pursue professional and research interest in the area of men's issues, particularly relevant to the overall health of the African American community. He has written several articles related to this interest, such as "A Theodicity that Speaks to the Suffering of African American Males," and is presently working on a manuscript entitled "Recovery and Liberation," about African American men in recovery from chemical abuse and dependency.

Introduction

James Newton Poling
Christie Cozad Neuger

We were invited by Marie Fortune to co-edit a special volume on "Men's Work in Preventing Violence Against Women." We wrote to a number of scholars who are doing research on the religious issues of this topic and asked them to reflect on their current work. All of these men and one woman are concerned about men working in partnership with women on a whole range of issues, including issues of domestic violence and sexual assault. We encouraged them to think about their work in relation to this topic and ask the following questions.

- Where in your experience and social world have you seen creative partnerships of men and women that have made a difference?
- Where have you seen men in counseling struggling with how to change their views on gender so they can become reliable allies with women and join the struggle to end violence against women?
- What creative thoughts have you had about how religion can become a resource for men who are working to change themselves into allies of women?
- What strategies do you see men using to help end violence by men against women?

[Haworth co-indexing entry note]: "Introduction." Poling, James Newton, and Christie Cozad Neuger. Co-published simultaneously in *Journal of Religion & Abuse* (The Haworth Pastoral Press, an imprint of The Haworth Press, Inc.) Vol. 4, No. 3, 2002, pp. 1-3; and: *Men's Work in Preventing Violence Against Women* (ed: James Newton Poling, and Christie Cozad Neuger) The Haworth Pastoral Press, an imprint of The Haworth Press, Inc., 2002, pp. 1-3. Single or multiple copies of this article are available for a fee from The Haworth Document Delivery Service [1-800-HAWORTH, 9:00 a.m. - 5:00 p.m. (EST). E-mail address: docdelivery@haworthpress.com].

10.1300/J154v4n03_01

In this publication, we focus on partnerships between men and women who share a common commitment to ending violence against women. What is men's work to end violence against women? What are men doing in various settings to confront violence against women? What are the religious resources that can empower men to work with women to end violence against women?

Men's work in the movement to end violence against women is a topic with much literature available in the secular discussion. Changing gender expectations and norms as well as sexual and domestic violence are favorite topics in the popular media. However, in religious circles, these topics are still regarded by many as novel.

In both religious and secular settings, most of the work to end violence against women continues to be done by women: survivors who have become activists, and women advocates who have been touched by the witness of survivors. Anyone who works in the movement immediately notices the gender asymmetry in who does the work. Many male religious leaders continue to say, "No one comes to me with this problem," in spite of overwhelming evidence of the violence in their own communities. Motivating and educating more men to join the everyday work of domestic violence shelters, rape crisis counseling, and child and abuse prevention, is an urgent matter.

Accountability is the key word in much of the literature by and about men who work at ending violence against women. In order to be trustworthy allies with women, men need to entrust their understanding and behaviors to women who are veterans of the movements. The need for male accountability to women is based on the assumption that women experience and understand violence in a more profound way than most men who tend to underestimate the danger facing women. Men who are willing to be accountable become important allies in the movement to make society safe for everyone.

Religion has a crucial role to play in motivating and educating men to do their share of the work. We must confront negative religious messages such as the headship of men in family and church, the complementarity of the sexes, exclusive male views of God, men's right to chastise women and children physically in order to "control" them, and other doctrines, as well as racial and class inequalities. We must confront religious beliefs and practices whenever they prescribe stereotypical gender roles that prevent men from having empathy with survivors who have experienced violence.

We anticipate that this is one of several publications that will address the issues of men's partnership with women in ending violence against women. We encourage all readers to submit articles on this and other subjects related to religion and abuse.

Jewish Men and Jewish Male Violence

Paul Kivel

SUMMARY. In this article, the author discusses the issues of male violence in Jewish families using a personal example and suggests resources in the Jewish tradition that can help to prevent male violence against women and children. He suggests that men begin with examining themselves, their family roles, and their leadership in the community as a way of reducing violence against women. *[Article copies available for a fee from The Haworth Document Delivery Service: 1-800-HAWORTH. E-mail address: <docdelivery@haworthpress.com> Website: <http://www.HaworthPress.com> © 2002 by The Haworth Press, Inc. All rights reserved.]*

KEYWORDS. Sexual and domestic violence, families, Jewish religion, male identity

After I had written *Men's Work*, a book on male violence, and after I had worked with incest offenders and batterers and had even said that I am never surprised to learn that any man is a batterer or child molester, my sister revealed to my mother and me that my father had molested her many times when she was a child.

I had conflicting feelings. I believed her. And, at the same time, I wanted to believe that there was some mistake, or that the abuse wasn't as serious as she described it, or that there were, somehow in a way I

[Haworth co-indexing entry note]: "Jewish Men and Jewish Male Violence." Kivel, Paul. Co-published simultaneously in *Journal of Religion & Abuse* (The Haworth Pastoral Press, an imprint of The Haworth Press, Inc.) Vol. 4, No. 3, 2002, pp. 5-13; and: *Men's Work in Preventing Violence Against Women* (ed: James Newton Poling, and Christie Cozad Neuger) The Haworth Pastoral Press, an imprint of The Haworth Press, Inc., 2002, pp. 5-13. Single or multiple copies of this article are available for a fee from The Haworth Document Delivery Service [1-800-HAWORTH, 9:00 a.m. - 5:00 p.m. (EST). E-mail address: docdelivery@haworthpress.com].

5

couldn't even imagine, extenuating circumstances. I hoped there was some way that I could deny the abuse because it contradicted everything I had believed about our family life and my childhood. Of course incest was common. Of course ordinary men did it. Of course you never knew. But my own father?

I quickly realized that I couldn't deny it, that it was perfectly and unfortunately believable, and in fact, was quite consistent with everything I knew about my father, and what I knew about my sister and her life struggles. When my sister told some of our relatives about the abuse, they had the same responses but even more strongly than I had. My father had been successful, educated, Jewish, likable, and a contributor to the community. How could he possibly have molested his daughter?

As I supported my sister and dealt with my own anger, pain, and sadness over my father's abuse, I realized again how fundamental male violence is as a force which keeps systems of exploitation and violence in place. As I confronted the denial within myself and among my relatives, I realized again how thick are the layers of denial which keep us from confronting and stopping the violence.

What is the connection between Jewish men and domestic violence against Jewish women? Obviously we can start with the fact that many Jewish women are abused by Jewish men. Although in some circles Jewish men may have a reputation for making good husbands, for being mensches, those of us who grew up with abusive Jewish fathers, stepfathers, uncles, or other family members know that such positive stereotypes can be just as false and damaging as negative ones.

Many of us who are Jewish men also experienced physical, emotional, or sexual abuse from Jewish men. In addition, all men, including Jewish men, are likely to know women–our mothers, sisters, daughters, co-workers, partners, or friends–who have experienced violence, whether from Jewish or from non-Jewish men.

For all of these reasons this is not a Jewish "women's" issue, it is ours, as Jewish men. This is true regardless of how much we may want to deny or minimize the impact of Jewish male violence in our lives. However, this truth is also highly contested within our communities. Even for those of us who accept the reality of the devastating impact of male violence on our lives and on the lives of those around us, it can still be hard to admit that this is an issue of paramount importance–one in which we are morally and practically compelled to be involved.

Although we still face much denial within the Jewish community about the extent of male violence, many of us have come to understand the issues and to be, in the abstract, strong supporters of ending such violence. In actual practice, however, when it comes to men we know or know of, many of us inadvertently find ourselves denying, minimizing, or colluding with perpetrators of abuse and withholding support and resources for survivors.

For example, in the last few years there has been much conflict within parts of the Jewish community because many women have come forward accusing internationally known singer and spiritual leader Schlomo Carlbach of harassing and assaulting them throughout his over 30 years of leadership. It is hardly likely that all these accusations are false. Many women of various ages, from different parts of the United States who don't know each other have corroborated Carlbach's sexual abuse towards them. Yet even so, there has been denial and minimization about the charges from many Jewish men.

I know of rabbis, cantors, Jewish agency staff, Jewish summer camp staff, respected lay members of the Jewish community who also have abused others. In addition there are many thousands of ordinary Jewish men, Orthodox and Reform, Renewal, Reconstructionist and unaffiliated, who have physically, sexually, or emotionally abused their partners, co-workers, their children or their clients. Yes, Jewish men can be abusive–this is incontrovertible and today seldom denied in principle.

What is denied is that the particular Jewish man I know could be that abuser. Someone else's rabbi, someone else's father, someone else's good friend–they could be abusive. But my rabbi, my father, my good friend, my revered spiritual leader? Wait a minute, I've known him for years, he is so caring, he is so smart, he contributes so much, he has such insight and besides he's such a mensch–not the abusive type at all.

I have been in this situation of disbelief more than once myself. Given the wonderful contributions of Schlomo Carlbach to Jewish life and culture it was hard for me to believe he could have done the things he was accused of. A few years ago I found out that a good friend of mine had assaulted his partner. Yet, given the wonderful caring and deep insight I had experienced in my friend it was hard for me to believe he could have hit his partner. Even more painfully, given the experience I had of a loving family and happy childhood, I did not want to believe that my father had sexually molested my sister and had been verbally and emotionally abusive to my mother.

Each time I have been confronted with instances of male violence I have had to remind myself about how abusers operate–how charming, how manipulative, how discreet, how ordinary they can be. I have had to remind myself that people seldom make up stories of their victimization because coming forth as a survivor of abuse often sets them up for further abuse from the perpetrator, and, in addition, to public attack, disparagement and isolation. I have needed to remind myself that women are so discredited in the public eye, and men's word given so much authority that it will often just feel like I should believe his word against hers. I will also have to remind myself that the fact that he is abusive doesn't negate or lessen the contributions he might have made in other areas. Being a perpetrator of violence is only part of who he is–the other parts are still real and important to keep sight of. And so is the abuse. His contributions cannot negate that either.

Holding all these feelings and information has been difficult for me. The anger, the disappointment, the grief can be overwhelming and deeply uncomfortable. There is a "here we go again" cynicism that these revelations bring on in me because I know too well how ordinary and common abuse is in the Jewish community. There is a feeling of outrage at the perpetrator for the violence and betrayal because I know how devastating it is for the survivor, and for our community.

And I always feel equal parts hope and pessimism. Hope because I want to believe that this time the Jewish community will come together, believe the abused, and confront the perpetrator. Maybe this time we will move forward in our collective understanding of how and why abuse happens and how crucial it is that we respond with justice and compassion. And, of course, pessimism because I have yet to see such a response from any Jewish community I have worked with.

I have seen great individual courage and commitment as individuals, women and men, have reached out to survivors and offered them support, resources, advocacy, and healing. I have seen small groups of women establish shelters for Jewish women, advocacy programs, information booklets, training for Jewish leaders, and personal support networks. I have yet to see a congregation confront the stark and painful reality of male violence in the Jewish community with strong, comprehensive, sustained, and committed efforts to end it.

Instead I see abuse continue. Instead I hear excuses like these:

> "We can't just believe her word over his."
> "I can't believe he would do something like that."
> "She is just vindictive, angry, unhappy, controlling, or likes being a victim."
> "He says he is sorry."
> "The situation is too divisive for the community to deal with."
> "It's a private matter."

"It's all over now, they have separated/he's dead/it happened a long time ago."

Instead I see women avoiding services, or leaving the congregation, I see women leaving Judaism, I see women's connection to their religious practice and spiritual lives severed. I see other congregants (mostly women) become cynical and sometimes also leaving their congregation.

I see inadequate, victim-blaming responses to male violence from men and women alike. But as a man I want to address other men because I think we have a particular responsibility to respond to Jewish male violence, and we have often been the ones to most adamantly deny or minimize abusive situations, blame the abused or collude with the abuser.

A QUESTION FOR JEWISH MEN

My question is why do you think your friend is any different than my friend, your father different than my father, your spiritual leader different than mine?

If an abused person comes forward we need to attend to her or his needs for safety, healing, and justice. But all too often our attention is cursory and our efforts inadequate because we don't want to believe that the accusation is true. We don't really believe her so we go directly to the accused and ask him if it is true or not. If he says no we push to have the matter dropped. If he says "Yes, but it happened a long time ago," or "Yes, but I've changed since then," or "Yes, but I made an error in judgment," or "Yes, but I'll never do it again," or "Yes, but it was mutual–she was quite abusive to me" then we may still want to conclude the investigation and move on by minimizing the abuse, and downplaying its effects on the victim. Either way, we are relying on the word of someone whose abuse tactics often include denying, minimizing, or blaming others for their behavior. Abusers often simply lie and deny what they have done.

Taking male violence seriously means much more than asking an alleged abuser if they have been abusive. Knowing the levels of violence in Jewish family and interpersonal relationships we can no longer afford to be surprised by accusations of male violence, no matter how well-known, how respectable, how Jewish, how well-loved, or how close to us a man might be.

Every situation is different and we will still have to determine how best to meet the needs of the abused and of the community. We will still have to determine the most appropriate response to the perpetrator. But if we are not surprised we will notice the abuse more often; we will believe the survivors more seriously; and we will collude less with the men who perpetrate attacks on those around them. We will begin to end the silence that keeps the violence unchallenged.

In order for our personal responses to be stronger we need a systematic, community wide response that puts the safety and healing of survivors first, that provides training and education and prevention throughout the community, and then, finally, focuses on the perpetrator and his T'shuvah. Our goal should not be so much on just stopping violence, but on creating a safe, inclusive Jewish congregation/community in which every member is valued, fully able to participate, safe, and able to heal from abusive situations (with some obvious qualifications for people who are abusive). In order to achieve such a community, all of us who are Jewish men have some work to do.

WHAT IS JEWISH MEN'S WORK?

There are several aspects to Jewish men's work against male violence. First we need to look at our own behavior. In what ways are we controlling or abusive? How do we treat the people around us–our children, our partners, our co-workers, our neighbors? Are there any ways in which we scare, intimidate, threaten, yell, or coerce others using physical, emotional, psychological, sexual, or financial means? What are we going to do to change those patterns?

The second area of men's work is to challenge other men. Many of us know men who are abusive. Many of us see male intimidation, put-downs, and harassment occurring and do not intervene. Many of us hear of abuse and do not investigate. Many of us know of men who are abusive and we deny, minimize, or otherwise downplay the significance of the abuse. And many of us fall back on individual self righteousness, excusing our lack of involvement by saying that we are good men, we don't hit or abuse anyone and that's all we can be responsible for.

We do have a responsibility to stop male violence. The concept of Tikun Olam does not just apply to abstract social justice issues. It applies as well to interpersonal relationships. Part of men's work is to reach out to other men with strength and caring to challenge abusive behavior whenever and wherever we encounter it.

The third area of men's work is to model and teach our sons–Jewish boys and young men–non-abusive ways to be men. They are looking to us for models of men who treat others respectfully, solve problems non-violently, and participate in struggles to make our community more inclusive and more just. Many of us are fathers, others are teachers, counselors and therapists, probation officers, youth workers, coaches, uncles, grandfathers, older brothers and cousins and neighbors. We can reach out to Jewish boys and young men to help them understand and resist the pressure to become men who abuse others. Jewish youth receive the same mainstream cultural messages from peers and the media as Gentile youth do to be tough and aggressive, in control, not to back down, and to use force to take care of business. They also receive the cultural messages to devalue and objectify women and to expect them to take care of men emotionally and sexually. Drawing on our own values and on the progressive aspects of Jewish tradition we can contradict those messages and offer them other ways to be strong, caring, and involved Jewish men.

The final area of Jewish men's work is in the community. We can be active participants in the struggles in our congregations, our neighborhoods and in our cities for gender equality, social justice and an end to male violence. We can support the efforts of the many Jewish women who are already actively working to stop the violence. We can help change the policies and institutional practices which foster abuse. We can support training and prevention efforts in our congregations, schools, and youth programs.

I want to end with an example of Jewish men who are making a difference. Although Jewish men have been active in the movement to end male violence since the very beginning, it has only been in the last few years that we have addressed ourselves to issues of male violence in the Jewish community.

Several years ago, inspired by the women of Shalom Bayit and their efforts to challenge domestic violence in the Jewish communities of the San Francisco Bay Area, a group of us came together to create a group we called Gvarim: Bay Area Jewish Men Against Violence. We began to support Shalom Bayit's work, and to do education with youth and adults within the Bay Area Jewish community. Some of us were members of the Kehilla Community Synagogue, a Jewish Renewal congregation of which I am a member. We decided to work with the congregation, in collaboration with Shalom Bayit to develop policies and protocols to create a safe congregational community and to respond to those incidents of abuse which were brought to our attention.

Through this work I have seen men take initiative in supporting the efforts of Jewish women to create a safer community. Men who are fathers, men who are spiritual leaders, men who are synagogue board members, men who are teachers–men who understand their stake in building a safe and inclusive community. The congregation has been developing a set of protocols dealing with all aspects of male violence and some of these men are helping to craft it, to refine it, to lobby for it, and to implement pieces of it as appropriate situations arise.

These men are willing to struggle with their own issues of abuse, with the traditional denial within the Jewish community, and with the patterns of collusion and male bonding that have often undermined women's safety. Each of these men inspire me and give me hope that, working with women, we can indeed confront male violence within the Jewish community.

I invite you to join these efforts. We have a long history in Judaism of drawing on alternative versions of masculinity which are not based on the dominating and violent norms of the societies in which we lived (the mensch tradition). These alternative masculinities have valued learning, critical thinking, caring, concern for justice, and sensitivity to the needs of the community. However these same values have not always translated into non-controlling, non-abusive relationships with women, with children, and with each other. Now is the time to extend our male values to include taking a stand against male violence and building a safe, inclusive community in which everyone can thrive.

QUESTIONS FOR JEWISH MEN TO ASK OURSELVES

Do I yell at the people around me?

Do I tease, put down or belittle others?

Do family members of co-workers "walk on eggshells" when I get angry?

Do I physically touch women around me in ways that are sexual, intrusive, or disrespectful?

Do I threaten or intimidate my children or partner?

Do I talk louder than others, interrupt people, pull academic or professional rank, or otherwise try to control conversations, silence others, or increase my own status?

Have I ever hit, slapped, shoved, pushed, or used my body to threaten others?

Have I had sex with a partner when I knew they did not want to?

Have I seen abuse in my family or in relationships around me and have not intervened?

What is my next step in ending controlling and abusive behavior in my own life and in the lives of those around me?

Holding Christian Men Accountable
for Abusing Women

Al Miles

SUMMARY. Historically, the Christian church has excused men of faith who abuse their wives and girlfriends. Christian men who beat, cuss, rape, stalk, and even murder women have often escaped not only criminal justice, but also have not been held accountable for their crimes by Christian clergy and laity. In contrast, abused women have usually been blamed for their own victimization. The women are told by spiritual leaders and congregants that they themselves, through their actions and inactions, "provoke" the abuse and violence men perpetrate against them. This article examines incidents of woman-blaming, which are still prevalent within Christian congregations. Suggestions on how clergy and laity can better deal with Christian men who abuse their adult female intimate partners are also offered. *[Article copies available for a fee from The Haworth Document Delivery Service: 1-800-HAWORTH. E-mail address: <docdelivery@haworthpress.com> Website: <http://www.HaworthPress.com> © 2002 by The Haworth Press, Inc. All rights reserved.]*

KEYWORDS. Abuse, Christian men, clergy, domestic violence, laity, woman-blaming

---

[Haworth co-indexing entry note]: "Holding Christian Men Accountable for Abusing Women." Miles, Al. Co-published simultaneously in *Journal of Religion & Abuse* (The Haworth Pastoral Press, an imprint of The Haworth Press, Inc.) Vol. 4, No. 3, 2002, pp. 15-27; and: *Men's Work in Preventing Violence Against Women* (ed: James Newton Poling, and Christie Cozad Neuger) The Haworth Pastoral Press, an imprint of The Haworth Press, Inc., 2002, pp. 15-27. Single or multiple copies of this article are available for a fee from The Haworth Document Delivery Service [1-800-HAWORTH, 9:00 a.m. - 5:00 p.m. (EST). E-mail address: docdelivery@haworthpress.com].

INTRODUCTION

Women never cause the abuse and violence men perpetrate against them. A disturbing truth that should generate no further disagreement than the statement *Sunday follows Saturday*. And yet, when the author proclaims the former at domestic violence awareness trainings throughout the United States, male attendees strongly protest. They insist women who are abused and battered emotionally, physically, psychologically, sexually, spiritually, had to have done something to cause their male intimate partners to attack them. Women, we are told, have "razor sharp tongues which castrate and tear down men emotionally"; that women "deplete men's God-given authority with their constant nagging and disobedience"; and, we are told, that women fail to carry out their "duty to provide for men's sexual needs" (thus, according to some male Christians, men have the right to force themselves sexually upon their wives and girlfriends). Curiously, male clergy and laity rarely assign any of the blame for the abuse upon the individuals who cause all of it: male Christian perpetrators. Why?

A LONG AND UGLY HISTORY

Down through the ages, there have been several reasons why abusive Christian men have gotten away with the crime of domestic violence. Let us consider five of the most commonly used justifications: patriarchy, denial, sanctity of marriage, "demonizing" qualities of divorce, and male headship and female submission.

Patriarchy

The patriarchal system has certainly always been alive and well in Christianity. Both the Hebrew Bible and Christian Scriptures have an androcentric, or male-centered, perspective and emerge from patriarchal societies. Some texts, which actually are misogynist (women-hating), are lifted up to the exclusion of other texts that clearly affirm mutual respect between the sexes. Still other texts have been twisted–inadvertently and intentionally–to suggest that our loving and merciful God and Jesus Christ for some reason grant males authority and privilege over females. Because of all the above, men have received special dispensation from Christian clergy and laity alike to do whatever they desire with their wives, girlfriends, daughters, and all other females, without any fear of accountability.[1]

Denial

Christian clergy and laity are often lulled into inaction regarding situations of domestic violence within the church because of denial. Adhering to the naive and false belief that no true "man of God" would ever abuse his wife or girlfriend, spiritual leaders and parishioners unwittingly perpetuate the criminal and sinful behavior of violent Christian men.

TASHA AND PHIL'S STORY[2]

Tasha was a teacher at a Christian high school. Phil, her husband of fourteen years, controlled Tasha's every move. Claiming she was "mandated" by God to honor and obey all his commands, Phil ordered his wife to phone him every hour on the hour. It didn't matter what Tasha was involved in at the time–a parent/teacher conference, consultation with a co-worker, or even a meeting with the school's principal–Phil insisted that his wife "check in" with him each hour.

Verbal put-downs were the only compliments Phil offered Tasha. The self-proclaimed "man of God" constantly told his wife that she was "dumber than a jackass and twice as ugly," and that Tasha's weight made her the "perfect candidate to excel at sumo wrestling." Phil also regularly beat and sexually assaulted Tasha. He justified his criminal behavior by telling Tasha the punishment would help her become a "dutiful Christian wife."

Depressed and feeling suicidal, Tasha turned for help to members of her church. She had known many of the folks all thirty-four years of her life, was deeply loved by them, and she felt certain they would offer their support during her time of great need.

Tasha's assumption was not accurate.

Candidly disclosing to several church leaders and laity the violence Phil had perpetrated against her their entire marriage, Tasha discovered she herself was rebuked. Some parishioners told the battered wife she had to be mistaken about Phil. After all, they explained, no real Christian man would ever commit the sins she had accused her husband of committing. Other congregants outrightly blamed Tasha for her own victimization. They told the beleaguered wife that either she must not be submitting totally to the "God-ordained authority" Phil had over her, or that Tasha was somehow "provoking" her husband's anger.

No one in the congregation held Phil accountable for the sins he was committing. No one wanted to believe that a Christian man would inflict such terror upon the woman he had promised to forever love and respect. There was one particular reason why the parishioners did not want to accept Tasha's truth.

Phil was the senior pastor of their church.

According to the United States Surgeon General, domestic violence is the greatest single cause of injury among U.S. women, accounting for more emergency room visits than traffic accidents, muggings, and rape combined.[3] While a small percentage of men are also violated, the American Medical Association estimates that two million women in this country are assaulted by an intimate partner every year.[4] The actual numbers are probably much higher because victims often do not report attacks, fearing both the stigma associated with abuse and the threat of reprisal from perpetrators. In addition, a report published in July 2000 by the Justice Department's National Institute of Justice and the Department of Health and Human Services' Centers for Disease Control and Prevention states that nearly twenty-five percent of surveyed women say they have been raped and/or physically assaulted by a current or former spouse or partner at some time in their lives.[5] And these alarming statistics do not include many of the emotional, psychological, and spiritual tactics male perpetrators use to abuse their female victims.

By the sheer numbers alone, Christian clergy and churchgoers should realize a disturbing reality: Incidents of domestic violence are as likely to occur among couples worshiping in Christian congregations as occur in all other communities.

Sanctity of Marriage

In Christian traditions marriage between a woman and man is indeed a sacred covenant; an oath taken by two people before God and Christ usually in the presence of family, friends, and other well-wishers, to stay together until parted by death. As part of most Christian wedding ceremonies, the couple also vow to honor, love, respect, and be faithful and kind to one another.[6] The author of a letter written to all the Christian churches near the city of Ephesus (many scholars believe this person was the apostle Paul), comments on the holy and mysterious nature of this bond.

Submit to one another out of reverence for Christ. Wives, submit to your husbands as to the Lord. For the husband is the head of the wife as Christ is the head of the church, his body, of which he is the Savior. Now as the church submits to Christ, so also wives should submit to their husbands in everything. Husbands, love your wives, just as Christ loved the church and gave himself up for her to make her holy, cleansing her by the washing with water through the word, and to present her to himself as a radiant church, without stain or wrinkle or any other blemish, but holy and blameless. In this same way, husbands ought to love their wives as their own bodies. He who loves his wife loves himself. After all, no one ever hated his own body, but he feeds and cares for it, just as Christ does the church–for we are members of his body. "For this reason a man will leave his father and mother and be united to his wife, and the two will become one flesh." This is a profound mystery–but I am talking about Christ and the church. However, each one of you also must love his wife as he loves himself, and the wife must respect her husband. (Eph. 5:21-33 NIV)

Situations of domestic violence clearly stand outside of Paul's admonishments to Christian husbands concerning how they must treat their wives. A husband needs to love his wife as he loves himself, as Christ loves the church. Domestic violence disregards Paul's instructions and disrespects Christ and his church. Abuse also causes a great amount of damage to wives, children, and, ultimately, to the batterers themselves because perpetrators miss out on the many blessings God offers husbands and wives when both individuals commit to the biblical virtues of love and respect. Domestic violence is neither loving nor respectful, and Christians must resist following the traditional path many churchgoers take of labeling all marriages between Christians as "holy."[7]

Sadly, when a situation of domestic abuse between a Christian couple is disclosed, pastors and parishioners generally absolve the perpetrating husband of any responsibility for the crimes he has committed, and, instead, blame the victimized wife. "My ex-husband would preach this incredibly wonderful sermon on Sunday mornings, and then he'd beat, cuss, and rape me every Sunday afternoon," recalls Tasha, who was married fourteen years to her abusive husband, Phil, a Christian pastor. "He was two people wrapped up in one larger-than-life body: charismatic and loving out in public, but an evil monster at home."

Tasha divorced Phil in the year 2000. Within weeks following the dissolution, members of the church board called a congregation-wide special session. During this meeting it was decided that Tasha should find a new church home. "I just couldn't believe what I was witnessing," Tasha said. "My Christian husband, a pastor no less, abuses the hell out of me for fourteen years. He never denied doing it; in fact, he told the entire congregation his actions were for my own good, to make me become a better Christian wife. And yet, not one person in the church held Phil accountable for his sinful behavior. And, no one suggested he step down from his leadership role. They just told me to go elsewhere to worship."

To date, Phil remains the senior pastor of the church Tasha was asked to leave.[8]

"Demonizing" Qualities of Divorce

For many Christians, the sanctity of the marriage covenant is held in higher regard than the safety of a woman and her children. This is attested to by the phrase so often recited by Christian clergy and laity that "a marriage must be saved at all costs." Thus, despite the very real threat of undergoing further attacks and even death, Christian women who are abused by their husbands are instructed by church leaders and laity to obey, pray for, and stay with these violent men. If they decide instead to divorce their perpetrators, the women themselves often receive a reprimand. They are told by both clergy and churchgoers that the marriage covenant is sacred and must never be broken.

It must again be pointed out that the criminal and sinful behavior of an abusive Christian husband is rarely mentioned by either clergy or laity as the real reason why a battered Christian wife is seeking to have a marriage dissolved. Nevertheless, given the circumstances, she has every right to do so. The Christian Scriptures offer two circumstances under which divorce is approved: "unfaithfulness" and "desertion" (Refer to Matthew 5:32 and 19:9, and I Corinthians 7:10-16). In cases of domestic violence, the sacred vow of marriage, the chastity and "oneness" in God, is broken *not* by the victimized wife, but by her abusing husband. Many clergy and parishioners erroneously blame the wife for leaving her spouse. In reality, the batterer destroyed the marriage covenant when he chose to abuse his wife. In essence he "deserted" her whether or not he remains in the home–by his inappropriate emotional, psychological, and sexual behavior.[9]

Male Headship and Female Submission

Cemented solidly in the doctrine of many Christian denominations, the dualistic teachings of male headship and female submission have trapped millions of battered women in unhealthy and potentially lethal marriages with abusive Christian men. The concepts have also allowed men of faith to feel justified in their violation of women and children. Although a great number of biblical passages are used to support the timeworn patriarchy, in Christianity the scriptures most often cited to uphold male dominance are found in Ephesians 5:21-33. Taken as a whole, the verses offer clear instructions on how Christian husbands and wives are to treat one another. Mutual love and respect are the core ingredients of this sacred bond.

Unfortunately, over the centuries, the passages in Ephesians have been used to elevate the status of men and put women down. Seldom do clergy members or congregants discuss the fact that nine of the twelve verses carry instructions for Christian husbands to follow. An inordinate amount of attention has been paid to what these verses tell wives, rather than what they demand of men. The passages clearly instruct husbands to love their wives as they do their own bodies. Nevertheless, the verses are often used to instruct women on what they are to do for their husbands–even those husbands who abuse their wives.[10]

Let us take a closer look at what "headship" meant in early Christian thought. The Greek word *kephale,* often translated as "head," has a number of metaphorical uses in the Christian Scriptures. Ordinarily it denotes "source," "origin," or "preeminence," rather than "authority over" or "ruler."[11] In an article addressing the classical concept of "head" as "source," Greek language scholar Catherine Clark Kroeger states:

> To declare that man was the source of woman, that she was bone of his bone and flesh of his flesh, was to give woman a nature like man's own. She was no longer of the substance of the animals but of man. She was a fit partner, his glory and his image. "Neither is the woman independent of the man nor the man of the woman in the Lord; for just as the woman is from the man, so man is from the woman, and all things are from God." (I Cor. 11:11-12)[12]

In the first century, the general Jewish and Greco-Roman understanding of marriage was that wives were to submit to their husbands in all things. Ephesians 5:24 reads, "Just as the church is subject to Christ, so also wives ought to be, in everything, to their husbands" (NRSV). But, as New Testament professor David Scholer points out, "[T]his cultural understanding of marriage is significantly qualified for those in Christ, so that the passage teaches an overarching concept of mutual submission. In this context, *kephale* hardly means 'authority over,' especially in the leadership and authority-bearing sense for husbands over wives. . . ."[13] What is clear, whether we are discussing first century or twenty-first century Christianity, is this: There is no justification for Christian husbands to abuse their wives in any way, at any time.

> Although the notion of husband as the head is often quoted nowadays as a justification for domestic violence, this is not the thrust of the New Testament passages. The headship image was to make both husband and wife part of the same body, dependent for their very existence upon one another. The husband was to view her not as attached to another family, but tenderly, as part of his own body, "bone of his bone and flesh of his flesh."[14]

Turning our attention to the concept of female submission, we find that abusive Christian men, clergy members, and churchgoers have all used the teachings to excuse men's violence and to blame women for their own victimization. Many of us who grew up in the Christian church were trained to think that Paul's famous instructions to husbands and wives in the book of Ephesians, chapter five, begins and ends with verse 22: "Wives, submit to your husbands as to the Lord" (NIV). Proclaimed by clergy and other pastoral ministers from pulpits and at weddings, and by parents, teachers, and other congregants as well, Ephesians 5:22 has established a foundation on which countless numbers of Christian marriages have been built.

The verse has also been a perfect setup for millions of women to suffer acts of domestic violence.

ARLENE AND ROBERT'S STORY[15]

For thirteen years, Arlene endured emotional and physical abuse from her husband, Robert, an ordained deacon in their church. According to Arlene, her husband was a little boy living in a man's body. "Like a spoiled kid left alone in a candy store, Robert was used to getting what he wanted whenever he wanted it," she stated. "Whether it was fancy sports cars, a new set of expensive golf clubs, or sex, my husband's desires were all that mattered to him."

When Arlene didn't consent immediately to Robert's demands, she said he would throw a temper tantrum. He'd call her many vile names and would also accuse her of not being a "loving Christian wife" because she wasn't willing to "please" him. This manipulative ploy nearly always worked. "I felt guilty for not being a better wife to my husband," confessed Arlene. "So, usually, I'd end up giving him whatever he was demanding at the time." However, there were times that Arlene said she refused to give in[16]. It was then that Robert began using physical force to get his way.

"My husband broke many of the bones in my body, gave me several concussions and punctured eardrums, and he left more black and blue marks on me than I care to remember," detailed Arlene. "He never once took responsibility for the violence he perpetrated. Instead, he'd tell me I was to blame for the abuse. 'If you'd only submit to my will,' he'd shout, 'then I wouldn't have to discipline you.' What real man of God would actually discipline his wife or treat her in such cruel ways?"

Paul's admonition in the book of Ephesians to Christian husbands and wives begins not at verse 22, but at verse 21: "Submit to one another out of reverence for Christ." Inclusion of this one sentence puts on a whole new light and brings clarity to the entire passage. No longer can Christians view marriage as a male hierarchical union. Instead, we are challenged to observe the covenant of matrimony like God and Christ intended: as a mutual and egalitarian bond.

The Greek word *hupotasso*, which is commonly translated as "to submit," has several different meanings. In fact, there are a cluster of words commonly understood to be related to "submission" in the Christian Scriptures: *hupotasso* (a verb meaning to submit, but also to behave responsibly toward another, to align oneself with, or to relate to another in a meaningful way); *hupotaktes* (an adjective meaning submissive, but more commonly, behaving in an orderly or proper fashion); *anupotaktos* (an adjective that is opposite to *hupotaktes:* disorderly, irresponsible, confused, or lacking meaning); and *hupotage* (a noun meaning submission, attachment, or copy).[17] In essence, Paul is instructing Christian husbands and wives to behave responsibly toward one another, align themselves and to relate to one another in a meaningful and respectful way. Thus, in Christian marriages, there must never be a hierarchical structure. Even when husbands are both loving and respectful, when there is no abuse whatsoever in the nuptial, male headship and female submission work against wives because this type of union disallows a woman to be a full and equal partner with her husband. The hierarchical structure is ultimately disadvantageous for husbands as well because it prevents them from reaping the benefits of sharing life with a woman who is equal to him in every way.

Most important, equality and mutuality in marriage, rather than female submission and male headship, help both women and men to live out the covenant God and Christ intended for Christians. There is no biblical justification for acts of domestic violence. Husbands have no right—not by God, Jesus, Scripture, beliefs, teachings, or tradition—to abuse their wives in any way. Equality and mutuality in marriage also help Christian women to understand it is never their duty, responsibility, or lot in life to have to endure the illegal and sinful actions of their Christian husbands, whether these inappropriate actions are emotional, physical, psychological, sexual, or spiritual in nature. Domestic violence is *always* worthy of condemnation.

HOW THE CHURCH MUST RESPOND
TO ABUSIVE CHRISTIAN MEN

If we are to deal effectively with Christian men who abuse their wives and girlfriends, church leaders and laity must do the following:

Make the safety of an abused woman and her children top priority. This is a vital first step in response to any situation of domestic violence. (Unfortunately, the top priority for many clergy and parishioners is to maintain the sanctity of the marriage covenant.) Ultimately, there are no foolproof plans to keep a wife totally safe from her abusive husband—whether or not that husband is confronted. Still, here are two things pastors and parishioners can do to enhance a wife's safety:

1. Never confront an abusive husband without thoroughly discussing with the wife both the benefits and the potential risks that such confrontation could bring. Get the wife's full permission before confronting the husband.
2. Make sure the wife has a safety plan (see below) that can be[18] implemented quickly should her husband's abuse continue or escalate.[19]

Help a victim establish a safety plan. Christian clergy and laity can assist a victim of abuse by helping her establish a safety plan. Include in this plan a safety kit, kept in a place where the perpetrator will not discover it, that contains items such as cash, a change of clothing, toiletries, an extra photo identification card, and a list of phone numbers of counselors, friends, pastors, and shelters.[20]

Seek education and training. If Christians are to play a vital part in helping a victim and perpetrator of domestic violence, then it is essential that we seek proper and ongoing education and training. We must keep updated on the articles, books, videos, and workshops that can help us become effective team members.[21] Concerning the latter, even with this training, we should never try to care for a victim or batterer alone. Instead, we must commit ourselves to working closely with community service providers, law enforcement officials, and members of the criminal justice system. These individuals also have a key role in victim safety and holding batterers accountable for the abuse they perpetrate.

Do not recommend couples' or marriage counseling. It is a common, but dangerous, mistake to suggest that a battered woman and her partner or husband seek couples' or marriage counseling. Domestic violence is *not* about men and women struggling as a couple. It is about the decision of one partner, usually the male, to use abusive and violent tactics to maintain power and control over his female intimate partner. Couples' or marriage counseling is inappropriate and risky, and could lead to further abuse and even death.[22]

Redirect a perpetrator's Scripture reading. For ongoing spiritual care, pastors need to set up with the abuser a reading schedule of passages from Scripture that teach equal value and dignity of husband and wife. Then pastor and abuser can discuss the larger theological dimensions of how God views men and women. That can counterbalance the tendency by abusers to misquote biblical texts to support male dominance. Here are a few passages to consider: Genesis 1:26-28, I Corinthians 7:3-4 and 11:11-12, Galatians 5:13, Ephesians 5:21 and 5:25-33, and Philippians 2:3.[23]

Hold an abuser accountable. A perpetrator of domestic violence is deceitful and manipulative. He rarely takes responsibility for his destructive behavior, blaming instead alcohol, children, drugs, job stress, mood swings, Satan, and, especially, his victim.[24] Christian clergy and congregants must take special caution as not to be fooled by a batterer's claims of being "a man changed by God." We must be especially wary if the alleged divinely inspired change occurs over a short period of time, if the man shows little or no remorse for the damage he has caused, if the man attempts in any way to blame anyone or anything other than himself for the abuse, or if the man refuses to seek (or stay in) a batterers' intervention program. (Domestic violence has little to do with a man having problems managing his anger. Therefore, referring a perpetrator to an anger management program will not help him stop his abusive behavior.) If an abuser is not willing to commit himself to the difficult and long-term process required to affect lasting change, then he will never truly become a man "changed by God."[25]

CONCLUSION

Women never cause the abuse and violence men perpetrate against them. Never. If we, as a "body of Christ," are to effectively deal with situations of domestic violence occurring within our communities, Christian clergy and laity must first accept this truth. We must also accept the fact that no man–under any circumstance, at any time–has a right to beat, cuss, rape, stalk, or terrorize a woman in any other way. Domestic violence is not only sinful, it is also a crime. As Christians, we dishonor the high stature bestowed upon us by God and Christ when we blame women for the brutality men of faith inflict upon them. We also fall short of our call to justice when we fail to hold abusive Christian men accountable for their behavior. As followers of Christ, we need more of our nonabusive males to speak out against all the acts of violence men perpetrate against women. The time is long overdue for male clergy and parishioners to *silence* the many false justifications men have always used to violate their wives and girlfriends. Christian men must courageously join women in working against male violence–in and out of the church.

NOTES

1. Al Miles, *Violence In Families: What Every Christian Needs to Know* (Minneapolis: Augsburg Books, 2002), pp. 52-53.

2. A portion of this story is told in Al Miles, "Christians Beware!" *The Clergy Journal*, April 2002, pp. 17-18.

3. Domestic Abuse Project of Delaware County, "Here are some things you should know about domestic violence . . ." Available on-line at www.libertynet.org/-dapcd/, accessed August 14, 2001.

4. American Medical Association, "Facts about Domestic Violence." Available on-line at www.ama-assn.org/ama/pub/category/48OT.htmlaccessed August 11, 2001.

5. National Institute of Justice, "Intimate Partner Violence Is Examined in New Justice Department Report." Available on-line at www.ojp.usdojugov/prosrelease/2000nij00141.htm, accessed April 13, 2001.

6. Miles, *Violence In Families: What Every Christian Needs to Know*, p. 58.

7. Ibid., p. 59.

8. Miles, "Christians Beware!" p. 17.

9. Al Miles, *Domestic Violence: What Every Pastor Needs to Know* (Minneapolis: Fortress Press, 2000), pp. 43-44.

10. Miles, *Violence In Families: What Every Christian Needs to Know*, p. 69.

11. Catherine Clark Kroeger, "God's Purpose in the Midst of Human Sin," in *Women, Abuse, and the Bible*, eds. Catherine Clark Kroeger and James R. Beck (Grand Rapids, Michigan: Baker Books, 1996), p. 207.

12. Catherine Clark Kroeger, "The Classical Concept of 'Head' as 'Source,'" in Gretchen Gaebelein Hull, *Equal to Serve* (Grand Rapids, Michigan: Baker Books, 1987), p. 278.

13. David M. Scholer, "The Evangelical Debate over Biblical 'Headship,'" in *Women, Abuse, and the Bible*, p. 43.

14. Kroeger in Hull, *Equal to Serve*, p. 282.

15. A portion of this story is told in Al Miles, "Domestic Violence: Helping More Clergy Become Involved in the Care of Victims," *The Clergy Journal*, August 2000, pp. 37-38.

16. Miles, *Violence In Families: What Every Christian Needs to Know*, p. 71.

17. Catherine Clark Kroeger, "Let's Look Again at the Biblical Concept of Submission," in *Violence against Women and Children*, eds. Carol J. Adams and Marie M. Fortune (New York: Continuum, 1995), p. 136.

18. Miles, *Violence In Families: What Every Christian Needs to Know*, p. 73.

19. Al Miles, "When Words Abuse," *Leadership*, Spring 1999, pp. 99-100.

20. Ibid., p. 99.

21. Miles, *Violence In Families: What Every Christian Needs to Know*, p. 47.

22. Ibid., pp. 46-47.

23. Miles, "When Words Abuse," 100.

24. Ibid.

25. Miles, *Violence In Families: What Every Christian Needs to Know*, pp. 41-42.

Infinite Responsibility:
A Shared Experience of Batterers
and Those Who Treat Batterers

David Livingston

SUMMARY. In this article, the author explores his experience of working in a rehabilitation group for men who batter women, examining the problem of frustration with the processes of change for batterers and counselors. As men change, they feel a sense of increasing responsibility as they seek new ways of relating to women. He adapts the insights of Levina's levels of moral responsibility that can provide insight and support for men through the change process. *[Article copies available for a fee from The Haworth Document Delivery Service: 1-800-HAWORTH. E-mail address: <docdelivery@haworthpress.com> Website: <http://www.HaworthPress.com> © 2002 by The Haworth Press, Inc. All rights reserved.]*

KEYWORDS. Sexual and domestic violence, responsibility, male identity

In the Brothers Karamazov, Dostoyevsky states, "We are all responsible for all, for all men before all, and I more than all the others."[1] Emmanuel Levinas uses this quote as a foundation for amplifying the meaning of the experience of responsibility. In Levinas' own words, "The infinity of responsibility denotes not its actual immensity, but a re-

---

[Haworth co-indexing entry note]: "Infinite Responsibility: A Shared Experience of Batterers and Those Who Treat Batterers." Livingston, David. Co-published simultaneously in *Journal of Religion & Abuse* (The Haworth Pastoral Press, an imprint of The Haworth Press, Inc.) Vol. 4, No. 3, 2002, pp. 29-41; and: *Men's Work in Preventing Violence Against Women* (ed: James Newton Poling, and Christie Cozad Neuger) The Haworth Pastoral Press, an imprint of The Haworth Press, Inc., 2002, pp. 29-41. Single or multiple copies of this article are available for a fee from The Haworth Document Delivery Service [1-800-HAWORTH, 9:00 a.m. - 5:00 p.m. (EST). E-mail address: docdelivery@haworthpress.com].

10.1300/J154v4n03_04

sponsibility increasing in the measure that it is assumed, duties become greater in the measure they are accomplished. The better I accomplish my duty the fewer rights I have, the more I am just the more guilty I become."[2] This has been the religious experience I have had working with violent men. The more I work with these men, the more I discover my own responsibility to them as well as my own culpability in a system that remains fundamentally irresponsible. Yet, if Levinas is right, then a sense of unattainability, both personally and socially, before the enormous burden of responsibility, is all we can ever expect to experience. It is similar to Christian eschatological language about the kingdom of God as hoped for but not yet present. The response to that which is hoped for is one of ongoing conversion. In working with violent men, I cannot do enough! The more I know, the more I recognize the distance between that which is sought and where I am. The more I achieve on my way toward justice the more guilty I become. This can be an overwhelming experience that leaves me feeling impotent and demoralized. At the same time, I find hope in the religious call to ongoing conversion, this call to respond to the demand of the other: the widow, the orphan, the broken, and the beaten, is a demand that can never be fulfilled and never be forgotten.

Men who work in the field of domestic violence experience varying levels of this overwhelming sense of responsibility. I have certainly felt this myself. As a white male theologian from a middle class suburban background, I find myself often distanced from some of the men in group. I have worked for a number of years with men who have been court ordered into treatment using the Duluth Model as the basis for the groups. I have been married for fifteen years and have no personal experience with violence in the home. Though I have no direct experience of violence, I have many memories from my childhood of struggling to understand what I now know to be emotional abuse by my father of my mother. These experiences allow me only a small window into the world of a violent home, and I continue to feel an inability, on many levels, to connect to the existential situation of the men in group. Over the years, I have found it easier and easier to find the language to begin the process of encountering these men where they are. It does present me with a sense of inadequacy and awe before the task of holding these men responsible and luring them toward a difficult process of conversion. It is not that women do not experience this responsibility, but men experience it differently because of their own complicity in the patriarchal system that has supported, and done much to create, the conditions under which violence against women is possible. In this paper, I wish to explore the often demoralizing experience of "infinite responsibility" that both batterers and teachers/counselors[3] who work with batterers encounter as they work in the field of domestic violence.[4] Secondly, I wish to show the parallels that exist between the batterers' experience of responsibility and the teacher's/counselor's experience of responsibility. I will then turn to the religious nature of responsibility as it is experienced by both groups. I will conclude with a recognition of the need for communal support as one attempts to live in a responsible manner in relation to the call of infinite responsibility. I will suggest that only within a community of support is ongoing work in this field possible, for the goal of the work is ultimately impossible to accomplish.

THE INFINITY OF RESPONSIBILITY

The first step in this attempt to uncover the existential experience of working with violent men is to explore the nature of encountering the other and the experience of responsibility to that other. In order to explain this phenomenon, I will draw on the work of Emmanuel Levinas as a figure who has articulated the core phenomenon of encountering the other and its concomitant responsibility.[5] The encounter with the other has been a central concern of both philosophers and theologians of the twentieth century. Hegel, Kierkegaard, Barth, Derrida et al. have asked, what does it mean to be truly other?[6] Violence itself has been understood phenomenologically and linguistically as denying the otherness of the other.[7] What this means will make perfect sense to those in the field of domestic violence, even if they have never read any continental philosophy once the terms other and face are more clearly defined below.

The face is used by Levinas as a term that connotes the otherness of the other. It is not the actual face of a person, but rather, the face is the phenomenon of an encounter that calls us to recognize the person before us as a person that is genuinely different than we are. The face of the other demands that we recognize that this is a person we cannot control. The face is that which cannot be contained within any system of thought or any "box" that we wish to put it within. The otherness of the other, which is always beyond any encapsulation that I may want to make of him/her, is the defining characteristic of the face. Responsibility is the felt obligation that I have to the face. The face demands of me that I recognize it as other and do no violence to it. The face is vulnerable and it is the vulnerability of the face that calls me to responsibility. This recognition, according to Levinas, is codified in the prohibition "thou shall not murder." In this phrase we put in words what the face demands from us in a pre-linguistic moment of encounter.[8] When we are confronted with difference or otherness we often seek two opposing responses: One is to annihilate that which is different and the second is to assimilate the otherness into the whole or into our self. The very nature of difference does not allow the second, for if it is genuinely different it cannot be assimilated.[9] The option of destroying the other is where the prohibition against murder begins. We do not seek to destroy that which is our self nor do we seek to murder that which is merely an object, but that which has the characteristics of genuine otherness we seek to control, to bring within our own world, to bring within "the totality." And, when we cannot assimilate the otherness of the other, and this other person continues to tug, pull, or push against us, the use of violence to destroy the other becomes one of the prevailing responses. Anyone who has worked with violent offenders, especially those who have worked with batterers, recognize this phenomenological explanation of the desire for control, because it is the lived experience of the men with which we work. What Levinas offers is a phenomenological description which opens up a means of analysis that helps to understand not only a man who violates his partner, but also to understand ourselves as we attempt to work with these men.

Most people who have worked with batterers understand that one of the central dynamics of domestic violence is the desire to control one's partner by the batterer, but what of the relationship between the counselors/teachers and the batterers. There is an equally powerful tendency to want to destroy or assimilate the batterers on the part of society. There are many in society that would wish nothing less than the destruction of perpetrators of violence. The death penalty is certainly the most clear example of this, but castration of pedophiles, desired vengeance toward all perpetrators, and the get tough on criminals attitude; all represent this desire to destroy perpetrators. Though most people who work with offenders tend to be able to see beyond this tendency for destruction, the teacher/counselor is likely to want the batterer to think like the teacher/counselor thinks. It is the goal of most programs to have the batterer see things the way "we" see them, and to have him understand and live according to the curriculum. This may seem very benign, but it has a certain level of violence inherent within it, as many who have worked in this field know all too well. When in the midst of a group or counseling session, one encounters a man who is belligerent and refuses to cooperate, one wishes nothing more than to throw him out of group, call his probation officer or threaten him with some consequence in order to bring him back into that totality, which we call appropriate group behavior. It is very difficult to accept that he does not see a woman as a person, that he cannot recognize her face. Yet we so wish for him to see things as we do, that we must bring him back into this way of thinking with force if necessary. Here in lies the paradox. How do we teach a batterer to recognize the face of his partner if we, as teacher/counselor, refuse to recognize him as an other, if we refuse to recognize his face?

I am not attempting to say that we should just sit back and let men view their partners as objects to be controlled, but I am pointing out that it is not a simple matter of forcing the batterer into conformity with "our" presuppositions of equality and respect. Instead, we need to try to model recognizing the face of the other as we coax these men into a position where they can also see the face of the other. It is a very difficult position to be in, and one that all those who have counseled violent men recognize as an experience of encountering a goal that cannot be achieved. It is an example of infinite responsibility in the same way the men experience infinite responsibility toward the survivor of their violence.

ASYMMETRY AS AN ASPECT OF THE ETHICAL RELATION

Let me be more clear by discussing what Levinas calls the asymmetry of the experience of responsibility. One of the criticisms that is often leveled against Levinas is that he denies the mutuality of the ethical relation and instead calls for a recognition of the basic asymmetry of all ethical relations.[10] This is an important insight for those who have worked with batterers. What Levinas means by an asymmetrical relationship is one that is not balanced. The relationship is not defined by mutual responsibilities or expectations, instead the relationship of responsibility is defined as one-sided. I only know that I owe you. I only know that I am responsible to you. What you owe to me is not something that I can know or claim as a balancing force. This is what Levinas means by an asymmetrical relationship, and he believes every encounter with the face calls forth a sense of responsibility and further that all experiences of responsibility are asymmetrical.

Batterers are frustrated by this asymmetrical relationship of responsibility. Most, if not all, would not understand the language of asymmetry, but if it was stated to them in different terms, they would certainly understand. For example, men certainly understand that as men guilty of assault, they are expected to not speak to the victim of their assault, they are not to see her, they must pay for her hospitalization, they must pay for child support, and they must attend twenty-six weeks of batterer's treatment. In addition, the man convicted of assaulting his partner is to go through a long and difficult process of changing his attitudes while he sees that she is not required to do anything or to change in any way. Put in these terms, the man convicted of assault will clearly understand what is meant by asymmetry. This is not an attempt to justify the anger and frustration of these men, rather it is an attempt to understand why men's experience of responsibility to their partner is one of an overwhelming burden. It is a description of what responsibility demands. Responsibility, by its very nature, is asymmetrical. It is not a relationship in which both owe to each other. The refrain of Levinas returns, " . . . the better I accomplish my duties the fewer rights I have, the more I am just the more guilty I become."[11] Put in terms of domestic violence, I owe my abused partner respect, reparations, and safety. She owes me nothing. That is to say, the reality of my responsibility is in no way dependent upon whether she takes up her own responsibility. In fact, the more a batterer comes to understand the extent of what it means to respect his partner as an equal, the more personal work he will realize still needs to be done.

Batterers are not the only persons who experience this asymmetrical relationship. Teachers/counselors of violent men also experience this asymmetry in their relationship with the perpetrators of violence. If I avoid the desire to assimilate or destroy the batterer, which I have committed to do when I took on this work, I must be willing to encounter the "face" of the batterer. The more I realize how much I owe to each batterer, the more I realize that I will never be able to respond adequately to the call issued by his "face." Though I feel inadequate before the task, it is equally impossible to just walk away from this issue. If the violence is going to stop, then he must be treated as a person, and in order to do that there must be a place that will hold him accountable while at the same time validating his humanity. Making a similar point in *I and Thou*, Martin Buber states the following when describing the one who truly encounters the face of the other. "He has, to be sure, abolished moral judgments for ever; the 'evil' man is simply one who is commended to him for greater responsibility, one more needy of love. . . ."[12] I am not suggesting that batterers are ontologically evil, but that those who destroy others, disregarding the face of the other, at the same time, call us to respond to our encounter with them by recognizing our responsibility to the face of the other in each of these encounters. We may wish to demonize the batterer or see him as an object to be controlled and manipulated, but this only furthers the cycle of violence.[13]

As teachers/counselors of batterers we experience an asymmetrical responsibility that is parallel to the batterer's experience of asymmetrical responsibility. It does not matter whether the batterer adopts an attitude of accountability and respect. I, as a counselor, still owe him respect. I am still responsible to help him to become a responsible self. I am responsible to teach him that his responsibility is asymmetrical and infinite in character, just as I am to embody my asymmetrical and infinite responsibility toward him. When men act in a threatening manner in group or attempt to collude with other men in order to blame the survivor of their violence, it draws out of me a desire to threaten him with my own authority. This only shows me my own inability to accept him as a face calling for greater responsibility. Each batterer may be encountered as an evil mask, as one who will not listen, one who will only attempt to manipulate, one who will never change his beliefs or behavior, and yet this one is the one I am responsible to. It is a very difficult road to walk, since it is true that many men who have been abusive are quite adroit at manipulation, deception, and coercion. Yet each of them is also more than this, and if we are to teach them how to see the face of the other, we must see them as an other and accept all the responsibilities that go along with recognizing the face of the other.

RESPONSIBILITY AS A RELIGIOUS EXPERIENCE

The task of responding to this infinite responsibility encountered in the face is a religious experience. The encounter of the face is the very core of the religious experience, according to Levinas. It is in the experience of unending and increasing responsibility that one experiences infinity. Both of these experiences, tied together as they are, evoke a sense of awe before that which is infinite. It is the experience of attempting to grasp that which always brushes past your outstretched hand and then lingers just beyond our reach before it disappears out of sight. There is enough contact to recognize it as real, and not merely an illusion, but one can never grasp it. This is very similar to the way in which people may speak of an encounter with the divine. The other becomes the source of mystery and infinity within our midst; it is the *mysterium tremendum* encountered in the face of the other. We have stated that the counselors experience their interactions with the batterer as experiences of infinite responsibility, as religious experiences. Additionally, it suggests that teaching abusive men to see the face of the other is an act of religious education. It may very well be that many men in group have always perceived every other person as a mere object and that group sessions are the first time they have been asked to ponder the infinite, that is, ponder the face of the other as other. Batterers' groups become a place where we continually are confronted with the infinite, with that which is beyond our grasp. The batterers in class or in therapy discuss their own desire for control as one of the central and enduring problems they face in their new life attempting to respect women. This desire for control is what reduces the face of the other to a mask or an object that can be manipulated, assimilated or destroyed. As teachers/counselors, we confront the same desire for control over the other in our encounters with the batterers. Religious life calls us beyond a life of control to a life in which we accept the mystery inherent in the encounter of the face of the other.

Being a religious person often involves more idolatry than genuine faith. It is far more common to objectify the divine than to experience the divine as an unfathomable mystery. One of the blind spots of many religious people is that they do not recognize that they are involved in idolatry as they practice their religion. Breaking out of our complacent idolatry is very difficult, but sometimes those who are different offer us a new perspective on our own practice. Meeting and talking with those who practice a different religious tradition often teaches us where our own religious practices are most idolatrous, as well as where they are the most genuine. The same can be said of teaching men about how to live in a healthy and respectful relationship with a partner. The teacher/counselor often discovers how regularly he treats his own partner and children as objects and how often he attempts to control his partner, while he is teaching the batterer about equality, power, and control. As with the batterer, the teacher/counselor discovers that his own relationships, all of them, are wrought with infinite responsibilities.

RESPONDING TO THE CALL OF INFINITE RESPONSIBILITY

How is one to respond to a call of responsibility that is infinite in nature? I realize that I cannot fulfill the demands of these relationships in any adequate way. I also realize that this responsibility is constantly increasing every time I try to fulfill it. I also realize that it is in the teaching/counseling of these men that I am most forcefully confronted with my own inadequacy. One response is to become disillusioned and over-whelmed by the insurmountability of the goal and so give up the work all together. This is represented by the constant threats of burnout within the "service" professions. Another response is to continue to do the work thinking, in a naïve manner according to Levinas, that some day I will actually fulfill my responsibility. A third option is that I can continue to do the work recognizing that I will never accomplish my re-sponsibility to any of my relationships, but recognizing it as a religious journey in which the doing of the work is the goal. If I choose the third option, then I certainly cannot perform this work alone. Any religious act must be done in community. Any ethical act can only be maintained in community.

Sharon Welch powerfully demonstrates in her book *A Feminist Ethic of Risk*, the importance of community when one is struggling against entrenched social problems.[14] Welch is primarily addressing issues of racism in her text, but her insight remains appropriate to our discussion. The patriarchy which stands as the foundation beneath domestic vio-lence is as entrenched within the social structures of contemporary American culture as any other entrenched ideology supporting a social ill. When facing issues of this kind, Welch points out that discourage-ment and an eventual dissipation of commitment are to be expected. If one attempts to work on issues such as domestic violence alone, one will eventually run out of energy and motivation as one sees the same level of abuse and often the same abusers. Recidivism is very high for the clients, but returning over and over to group for the teacher/coun-selor is not an easy discipline to maintain. Welch finds this all too often the case among middle class social activists. Over time the pull of the conformist society is so strong that people leave the cause and become a part of the larger society that accepts the inevitability of the injustice, without remaining a critic of the injustices.

To avoid this assimilation into the fabric of a society unwilling or un-able to be responsible, one needs a community which will urge you on when you are unable to continue in your protest. This is certainly true of people who work in the field of domestic violence. It is very difficult to maintain one's commitment to working with batterers when one sees so little change. Recidivism rates remains high and every year or two one of the men in group or in therapy is likely to kill his partner and then commit suicide. This does not breed loyalty and commitment, but rather discouragement and hopelessness. It is what Welch calls an "ethic of cultured despair" which she defines as having the two following charac-teristics: "(1) the despair is cultured in the sense of its erudite awareness of the extent and complexity of many forms of injustice; and (2) the knowledge of the extent of injustice is accompanied by despair, in the sense of being unable to act in defiance of that injustice."[15] I have in some respects painted a picture of cultured despair toward the entrenched social problem of battering and so I turn to Welch for a possible remedy. Welch calls for a critical theology of liberation. This theology calls for a celebration of limits, contingency, and ambiguity.[16] In her analysis of the need for recognizing our own limits and contingency as well as the ambiguity of all ethical work, she is critical of Levinas precisely because of the asymmetry of his ethics. She sees no ability to form community since every relation is always uni-directional and therefore one can never expect to receive anything back from any relationship. This may be overstating Levinas's point, but it is an important reminder that though responsibility may be asymmetrical, relationships of friendship and community must be based in mutuality and are not asymmetrical. Welch states that only in a community that supports each member as they become discouraged, is an ongoing resistance to oppression possible. For Welch, this is also a religious act, but the divine is not a receding reality always an infinite distance away, in Welch's words, "Divinity is not a mark of that which is other than the finite. Grace is not that which comes from outside to transform the conditions of finitude. Divinity, or grace, is the resilient, fragile, healing power of finitude itself. The terms holy and divine denote a quality of being within the web of life, a process of healing relationship, and they denote the quality of being worthy of honor, love, respect, and affirmation."[17] In this quote one finds a common element between Welch and Levinas, that the divine or the holy reside in the affirmation and respect of the other. This experience of the divine is always more absent than present for Levinas. In contrast, the divine is present in the mundane everydayness of encounter for Welch, but in both cases it is the ambiguous encounter with the face of the other that allows us to recognize the divine. What Welch adds to our discussion is the clear need for community. Levinas had left us alone and Welch offers us community as we struggle to respond to the infinite responsibility we encounter in the face of the other.

SUPPORT FOR THE SISYPHUSIAN HERO

I wish to close this essay with an image that represents both the worker in the field of domestic violence and the batterer, that is the figure of Sisyphus rolling his rock. Sisyphus becomes the hero of the person who works in batterer's treatment as well as for the batterer. Sisyphus was faced with a task that could never be finished. Worse still, Sisyphus always experienced his work as undoing itself. This is the experience of infinite responsibility that the batterer feels. I become more guilty the more I become just. I see myself as more controlling the more I understand controlling behavior. The more I see my partner as an other, as a person with her own dreams, goals, and desires, the more I realize how much I have harmed her. The teacher/counselor can say the same thing of his own relationships with his partner and children caused by his teaching of violent men. The teacher/counselor is also confronted with the face of the batterer. This face demands that the teacher/counselor treat him with respect even if the batterer returns each act of respect with abuse and manipulation.

It should be clear why Sisyphus is the role model. He is willing to roll the rock up the hill even if when he is sure that it will roll back down. One needs to be willing to continue to work with batterers even if one is sure that the batterer will return to his battering. Camus discusses the role of Sisyphus in the culture and ends his essay on the Myth of Sisyphus with the following proclamation: "I leave Sisyphus at the foot of the mountain! One always finds one's burden again. But Sisyphus teaches the higher fidelity that negates the gods and raises rocks. He too concludes that all is well."[18] Considering Sisyphus as pleased is a way of finding hope in infinite responsibility. It is a religious stance before the divine that is both present and absent in our encounter with the face of the other. Though Camus, like Levinas, leaves Sisyphus alone on his mountain, I prefer to think of Sisyphus gaining comfort by scanning the horizon and seeing hundreds of others pushing their own rocks. An even more comforting image, one which Welch's perspective supports, is to imagine that many of us work together to push the same boulder to the top of the hill and we are able to console each other as we watch the boulder roll back down to the bottom.

What we have come to now is that the batterer and the teacher/counselor share a great deal in common. Both face an infinite responsibility. Both have Sisyphus as their hero, and both, we hope, can face the task with a sense of deep happiness. As Camus says, "The struggle itself toward the heights is enough to fill a man's heart. One must imagine Sisyphus happy."[19] If we as teachers and counselors of violent men can approach these men with a greater sense of solidarity, I believe it will serve us all well. Recognizing that there are so many similarities between the often debilitating experience of infinite responsibility, may offer to the teacher/counselor a greater appreciation for what the violent offender goes through as he begins to genuinely see the face of his partner. This is not an easy journey, and when we fail to recognize how difficult it actually is to respond to an infinite responsibility, we fail in our responsibility to the violent men we seek to help. We must imagine Sisyphus happy.

NOTES

1. Fydor Dostevsky, *The Brothers Karamazov*, translated by Constance Garnett, New York: New American Library, 1957, p. 264. Cited in Emmanuel Levinas, *Ethics and Infinity*, translated by Richard A. Cohen, Pittsburgh: Duquesne University Press, 1985, p. 98.

2. Emmanuel Levinas, *Totality and Infinity*, translated by Alphonso Lingis, Pittsburgh: Duquesne University Press, 1969, p. 244.

3. I will use "teacher/counselor" throughout the text because the field of batterer's treatment involves both educational groups in which teachers attempt to address cognitive behavioral therapeutic goals and counseling sessions in which professional psychologists, social workers, and psychiatrists work with men to modify their behavior and their psyche. I have spent many years in the teacher role in a program that used the Duluth curriculum.

4. Levinas, *Totality and Infinity*, p. 199.

5. Levinas addresses this in all of his writing, but specifically in *Totality and Infinity*. For a more accessible introduction to the work of Levinas, see Ethics and Infinity, which is an interview with Philippe Nemo.

6. See Soren Kierkegaard, *Fear and Trembling: Dialectical Lyric*, edited and translated by Howard V. Hong and Edna H. Hong, Princeton: Princeton University Press, 1983; Friedrich Hegel, *Phenomenology of Spirit,* translated by A. V. Miller, Oxford: Oxford University Press, 1977; Jaques Derrida, *Writing and Difference*, translated by Alan Bass, Chicago: University of Chicago Press, 1978; and Karl Barth, *Church Dogmatics*, 14 volumes, Edinburgh: T & T Clark, 1958.

7. Jaques Derrida, *Writing and Difference*, translated by Alan Bass, Chicago: University of Chicago Press, 1978.

8. Levinas, *Totality and Infinity*, pp. 198-199.

9. This is something that Hegel's entire philosophical project attempts to explain. Hegel's dialectical thought is an attempt to bring together into a synthesis that which is truly other. One finds this most clearly articulated in the *Phenomenology of Spirit,* translated by A. V. Miller, Oxford: Oxford University Press, 1977.

10. Tina Chanter, *Feminist Interpretations of Emmanuel Levinas*, University Park, Pennsylvania: The Pennsylvania University Press, 2001. This volume is very critical in many of its essays on Levinas' unwillingness to engage issues of justice and mutuality. One finds a particularly clear criticism of Levinas in the essay by Luce Irigary entitled "The Fecundity of Caress: A reading of Levinas, Totality and Infinity, "Phenomenology of Eros"" reprinted in this collection on pages 119-144.

11. Levinas, *Totality and Infinity*, p. 244.

12. Martin Buber, *I and Thou*, translated by Ronald Gregor Smith, New York: Macmillan Publishing Company, 1987, p. 109.

13. There are some connections here to Girard's theory of reciprocal violence. Reciprocal violence creates an unending cycle of violence. See Rene Girard, *Violence and the Sacred*, translated by Patrick Gregory, Baltimore: Johns Hopkins Press, 1993, pp. 52-53.

14. Sharon Welch, *A Feminist Ethic of Risk*, Minneapolis: Fortress Press, 1990.

15. Ibid., p. 104.

16. Ibid., p. 158.

17. Ibid., p. 178.

18. Albert Camus, *The Myth of Sisyphus and Other Essays*, translated by Justin O'Brien, New York: Vintage International, 1955, p. 123.

19. Ibid., p. 123.

Premarital Preparation:
Generating Resistance to Marital Violence

Christie Cozad Neuger

SUMMARY. In this article, the author addresses the ministry of pre-marital counseling as a venue for preventing male violence against women. She criticizes current practices of premarital counseling for ig-noring male violence, and suggests alternative strategies for planning marriages and confronting couples with the realities of violence in relation-ships. *[Article copies available for a fee from The Haworth Document Delivery Service: 1-800-HAWORTH. E-mail address: <docdelivery@haworthpress.com> Website: <http://www.HaworthPress.com> © 2002 by The Haworth Press, Inc. All rights reserved.]*

KEYWORDS. Pastoral counseling, premarital counseling, sexual and domestic violence, marriage preparation

A VIGNETTE

At the wedding rehearsal, the bride and groom looked at each other and then at the pastor. "We kind of thought we'd like to leave the two in-dividual candles lit after we light the unity candle," the nervous groom said to the pastor. The pastor looked in a kindly way at the young man

[Haworth co-indexing entry note]: "Premarital Preparation: Generating Resistance to Marital Violence." Neuger, Christie Cozad. Co-published simultaneously in *Journal of Religion & Abuse* (The Haworth Pastoral Press, an imprint of The Haworth Press, Inc.) Vol. 4, No. 3, 2002, pp. 43-59; and: *Men's Work in Preventing Violence Against Women* (ed: James Newton Poling, and Christie Cozad Neuger) The Haworth Pastoral Press, an imprint of The Haworth Press, Inc., 2002, pp. 43-59. Single or multiple copies of this article are available for a fee from The Haworth Document Delivery Service [1-800-HAWORTH, 9:00 a.m. - 5:00 p.m. (EST). E-mail address: docdelivery@haworthpress.com].

10.1300/J154v4n03_05

and woman before him as he gently but firmly told them that this would not be possible. When the bride, gathering her courage, asked, "Why?" the minister said, "Because it's important to extinguish your own identity candles so that you can begin your new life as one person." He added, "And, it would ruin my wedding homily that's based on the mandate that two shall become one." The scene ended with the bride's parents telling the two young people to stop making a fuss because, after all, "pastor knows best."

I was present at the scene described above which was at a family wedding last winter. Having been involved, academically and pastorally, in the epidemic of partner battering over the past twenty years, I became interested in what the wedding rehearsal was communicating to this bride and groom about gender relations and, at some unarticulated level, about power, dominance, and, potentially, violence in this new marriage. And, I began to wonder what role pastors might play in premarital preparation and wedding planning that could serve as a counter-story of resistance against marital violence. Even though the wedding rehearsal I experienced last winter took place in a religiously conservative church and probably doesn't represent the norm of religious wedding services today[1], nonetheless there is very little evidence that religious leaders are taking an active stance in attempting to screen for, prevent, or create strategies of resistance against domestic violence. Whether it is in the general rhythms of ministry throughout the church, in premarital preparation, or in the construction of religious rituals, pastors have the obligation to actively do what they can to transform an environment that, at the least, tolerates wife battering and, at the worst, helps to normalize it.

THE CHALLENGES TO RELIGIOUS LEADERS

One of the problems I have found in talking with pastors is that they don't really believe that domestic violence is a serious problem, especially in their congregations. Therefore talking about intimate violence as "normal" may seem to be extreme.[2] It is clear that most religious leaders would prefer to believe that battering in intimate relationships is exceptional rather than normal. After all, most marriages in the United States occur because two individuals fall in love and desire to be good and caring partners with each other. Can't we assume that this motivation for marriage is an adequate antidote to domestic violence in most cases? We can't. Even in the context of love and well meaning intentions, the statistics about the occurrence of domestic violence force us to acknowledge its normalcy.

REALITIES OF DOMESTIC VIOLENCE

The United States Justice Department recently released a comprehensive study on the price of violence in our society. It attempted to include the costs of domestic violence and child abuse in addition to the kinds of violence more typically studied. The report found that "child abuse and domestic violence account for one-third of the total cost of crime."[3] A review of 3,676 records randomly selected from among female patients presenting with injury during one year, revealed that "40% of the women's injury episodes were identified as resulting from a deliberate assault by an intimate. Nineteen percent of the women had a previous history of abusive injury."[4] The American Medical Association estimates that four million women suffer severe assaults by boyfriends and husbands each year and that one in four women will be abused in her life. Estimates in a variety of studies range from two million to eight million women assaulted every year by partners and up to one in two women being abused sometime in her life.[5]

It is important for pastors to recognize and believe the statistics cited above. Until we accept that violence (both emotional and physical) is a part of a staggering number of the marriages in our congregations, we are unlikely to develop the courage and motivation it takes to be a counter-force against it, especially in the context of premarital preparation.

THE CENTRALITY OF GENDER ROLE SOCIALIZATION AND VULNERABILITY TO VIOLENCE

A second task for pastors is that they work to understand the role that gender socialization and power arrangements within gender have in setting the stage for violence. I want to make a case that a primary "story we live by" within which we make life decisions in this culture is a narrative that normalizes and even explicitly trains men to harm women in intimate relationships (especially when threatened) and women to find ways to interpret that violence such that they remain in it. I am not making this case in order to demonstrate hopelessness or an inevitable future of domestic violence. I describe these cultural narratives of violence in order that pastoral care ministries might be about the task of helping people (women and men, girls and boys) to examine the narratives by which they form and interpret interpersonal relationships and experiences of violence and to deconstruct and reformulate violence-laden narratives at both cultural and individual levels for the purposes of prevention and resistance.

Gender narratives in this culture are powerful and formative. They are binary and polarized. Women and men, girls and boys are defined over against each other. They are seen as opposites. This is one of the first harmful dimensions of gender stereotyping. Gender stereotypes teach girls and boys to relate to one another in ways so as not to challenge the power organization mandated by the dominant culture. Girls and boys begin their education to fit into the dominant narrative from the moment of birth in this culture. Along with their pink or blue hospital caps, they are talked to more or less, played with more or less, and given more or less freedom of movement as determined by their sex.

Girls' Gender Training

Lyn Brown and Carol Gilligan have documented that loss of voice seems to happen to many girls in late childhood/early adolescence. Gilligan and Brown did a longitudinal study of girls moving from age 8 into their early teen years. They found that younger girls were in significant relationships with their peers and would speak directly and clearly about violations and injustices done to themselves or to their friends. By the age of eleven these same girls were moving away from their own knowledge, using the phrase "I don't know" much more frequently and expressing implicit and explicit knowledge of the rules they were to follow in order to be acceptable and "in relationship." Gilligan and Brown summarize their findings by saying,

> At the crossroads of adolescence, the girls in our study describe a relational impasse that is familiar to many women: a paradoxical or dizzying sense of having to give up relationship for the sake of 'relationships.' Because of this taking of oneself out of relationship in order to protect oneself and have relationships forces an inner division or chasm, it makes a profound psychological shift . . . Women's psychological development within patriarchal societies and male-voiced cultures is inherently traumatic.[6]

Women and other members of non-dominant groups have thus learned to interpret their own stories and experiences, needs and goals, through the lenses of the other–those they have been taught to please and appease. Often they have lost access to their truths and their honest strengths.

Brown suggests that the girls learn, during early adolescence, what it means to be a "good" woman, fearing that if they don't follow the rules of "femininity," they will experience abandonment, exclusion, or ridicule. The recent publication of books of "rules" for how young women can attract men make these expectations explicit but my experience has been that girls and women, almost without exception, know what those rules are "by heart." And those rules about being feminine–quiet, nurturing, relational, supportive, full of caring feelings and empathy but rarely angry, etc.–teach girls and women how to be part of the "supporting cast" rather than actors or authors with voice and authority.

So, many young women learn in adolescence what it means to be a "good" woman and to "forget what they know." They give up the ability to be in authentic relationship for the sake of being related in ways that minimize the risks of exclusion and abandonment. This seems to be a mostly subtle process that most girls identify in a positive way–claiming in Gilligan and Brown's studies that their previous answers (from childhood) were "stupid" and that they see things more clearly as adolescents. Many of the young women in their study were able to identify a vague sense of disquiet, where they knew that if they expressed themselves honestly, especially in ways that might hurt other people's feelings, their relationships would be lost. Even when there was no evidence that the relationship in question was that fragile, the conviction that honest expression of feelings would lead to exclusion was maintained.

All of these developmental processes put women at risk for violence in male-female intimate relationships.

Boys' Gender Training

There has been a lot of important, gender-conscious research in the past ten or fifteen years about masculinity and men's psychological and spiritual health. This research has focused on the kinds of problems that may well be a direct result of their attempt to conform to male gender roles. Ron Levant writes that these new approaches to understanding masculinity "have provided a framework for a psychological approach to men and masculinity that questions traditional norms for the male role, such as the emphases on competition, status, toughness, and emotional stoicism and that views certain male problems (such as aggression and violence, homophobia, misogyny, detached fathering, and neglect of health) as unfortunate but predictable results of the male role socialization process."[7]

James O'Neill says that there are six patterns that are a result of gender socialization in men. Those are: (1) Restrictive emotionality; (2) Socialized control, power, and competition; (3) Homophobia; (4) Restrictive sexual and affective behavior; (5) Obsession with achievement and success; (6) Health care problems. He goes on to say, "also, how men are socialized produces sexist attitudes and behavior that explains much of the personal and institutional sexism in society."[8] O'Neill suggests that normative masculinity sets up persistent worries about personal achievement, competence, failure, status, upward mobility and wealth and career success in men's lives as well as a drive to obtain authority, dominance and influence over others. There is an emphasis on striving against others in competitive ways. Restrictive emotionality suggests that men have difficulty and fears about expressing feelings and difficulty finding words to express basic emotions. Ron Levant says that emotionality (and boy babies are more emotional than are girl babies) is socialized out of boys very intentionally, and this has four major consequences. First, boys develop a form of empathy that he calls 'action empathy' which is the ability to see things from another's point of view in order to predict what they will 'do' (not what they feel) and is usually employed in the service of the self (different from emotional empathy). Second, boys become strangers to their own emotional life and most develop at least a mild form of alexithymia (not having words for emotions). Men who are in the presence of an unrecognized emotion often experience only the bodily sensation of its physiological component. Third, boys pour their vulnerable emotions out through the channel of anger–one of the few emotions boys are encouraged to express. And, fourth, boys learn to channel their caring emotions through the channel of sexuality.

We need to recognize some of the important negative consequences for men of gender role strain. For example, probably all four of the gender role conflict factors correlate positively with depression in men and restrictive emotionality correlates positively with depression at all life stages of men. Higher levels of gender role conflict correlate positively with low self esteem. In race studies, men from Euro-American, African-American and Hispanic races all reported problems with success, power, and competition, restrictive emotionality, and conflicts between work and family relations. Results of several studies indicate strong correlations between gender role conflict and negative attitudes toward help-seeking.[9]

Other consequences include the fact that women live, on average, seven years longer than do men, and gender related lifestyle choices are part of these differences (e.g., between the ages of 15 and 24, men die at three times the rate of women mostly because of rates of violent death among male youth). Women are more prone to anxiety disorders and depression, but men show more evidence of anti-social personality disorder and alcohol and drug abuse.[10] And, men participate in violence in very destructive ways which can be clearly related to gender role training. In a recent study of 518 college men, 34% reported that they had engaged women in unwanted sexual contact, 20% reported they had attempted unwanted intercourse, 10% reported they had completed unwanted intercourse, and 46% said that they were at least somewhat likely to force sex if they wouldn't get caught.[11]

This leads us into the connections between gender training in a world that is ordered by dualistic power assignments and intimate violence in heterosexual intimate relationships.

IMPLICATIONS FOR MALE-FEMALE VIOLENCE IN INTIMATE RELATIONSHIPS

Women who stay in battering relationships, especially early on in the battering, tend to feel responsible for the relationship failure. There is debate in the literature about domestic abuse regarding how much self-blame women take on in a battering relationship but it does seem clear that for women who stay in the relationship and for women where the battering has not been going on for very long, self-blame is high. In addition, women in battering relationships tend to be and become depressed and to experience low self-esteem.[12] Certainly low self-esteem, which is the reality most closely tied to women's experience in battering relationships, is related to both a lack of entitlement and a lack of hope for creating something new.

And, women who are in battering relationships tend to look diligently for an explanation of a presumably aberrant situation–they engage in mind-reading. Lempert suggests that "violence is not a generally expected marital interaction. Cultural expectations of love and marriage do not include the 'stories from hell' that are the lived experiences of abused women. It is the unexpected nature of the violence, its seeming unpredictability, that makes it difficult to assimilate."[13] As a result, women look for an explanation that fits their core narrative. Piera Serra writes, "If the woman perceives the violence she is subjected to as the expression of her partner's inner world, and she considers the act as a symptom or a message, she will tend to disregard her own suffering and physical helplessness. Most of the women we interviewed who were still living with their partners interpreted their partners' violent behavior as a sign of distress."[14] The impact of this mind-reading and pro-other interpretation is that it gets in the way of moral evaluation and self-care. Psychologically, it also gives the woman the illusion that she still has a chance of fixing this problem in the relationship (which of course is not a problem in the relationship at all, but a problem in her spouse). Lempert suggests that "women in a battering relationship cannot afford to relinquish beliefs that they exercise some control, however minimal, over their lives because their survival depends on those beliefs and on continued use of whatever personal power they possess. With the erosion of these personal and social resources comes increasing demoralization."[15]

Serra concludes her discussion with the statement that women turn to outsiders to help end the violence so as to preserve the relationship. Yet most caregivers, whether police, clergy, counselors or friends, help only by suggesting that she leave the relationship–they do not feel they have the authority or right to make the batterer stop battering. Thus, when the batterer expresses contrition, mild affection, or even just temporarily ends the violence, she takes this as a sign of change and the bonding between them that may result is usually more satisfying than any outside help has been.[16] In this way, her training to be relationally responsible, to sacrifice self-interest for other care, and to hope for nurturing and love if she follows the gender rules are often temporarily met in the period between violent episodes by the batterer himself.

It is also important to look at men's gender training and its relationship to violence in marriages. The work of O'Neill and Pleck mentioned above begins to make some connections. Numerous studies have linked the inability to express vulnerable feelings with a strong tendency to engage in interpersonal violence. Other studies have made clear linkages between socialization for aggression and interpersonal violence.[17] And Paul Yelsma, in his work on intimate violence, named several factors which he called triggers for abuse in batterers. Those factors included: alcohol abuse; need to maintain authority; excessive need for control; high need for power; dependency conflicts; fear of intimacy; poor self-concept; witness of abusive behavior in family of origin; experience of abuse as a child; a tendency to label all emotions as anger; sex role rigidity; emotional inexpressiveness; intellectualizing of emotions; spouse specific non-assertiveness; tendency to experience suspicion and jealousy; social isolation; low levels of inclusion; and inexpressiveness and emotional dependency.[18] Obviously these factors are not all present in all men, and they take vastly different shapes depending on other particularities such as race, ethnicity, class, sexual orientation, and even age or place in the life cycle. Yet, as Wayne Ewing writes, "When the question is raised, 'Who is the male batterer?' the answer is sometimes given, 'Everyman!' Without pushing too quickly, let me simply point out here that this observation is accurate."[19] Numerous studies have shown that the psychological profiles of violent men (rapists or batterers) are not significantly different from the psychological profiles of the general population of men. Male gender training, which is facilitated by families and other important institutions, is related to high risk for interpersonal violence. In fact, Ewing goes on to say, "The teaching of violence is so pervasive, so totally a part of male experience, that I think it best to acknowledge this teaching as a civic, rather than as a cultural or as a social phenomenon. Certainly there are social institutions which form pieces of the total advocacy of violence: marriage and family; ecclesiastical institutions; schools; economic and corporate institutions; government and political institutions."[20] He concludes his article with the following statement, "I used to think that we simply tolerated and permitted male abusiveness in our society. I have now come to understand rather that we advocate physical violence. Violence is presented as effective. Violence is taught as the normal, appropriate and necessary behavior of power and control."[21]

The issues of power and hierarchy are a foundational part of understanding domestic violence. We must not fall into the mistake that many battered women make that battering is primarily a symptom of personal distress or dysfunction of her male partner. Michael Kaufman writes, "Men's violence against women is the most common form of direct, personalized violence in the lives of most adults and . . . is probably the clearest most straightforward expression of relative male and female power."[22] Joseph Pleck, who has been so instrumental in developing a new psychology of men, notes that men create hierarchies as a key component of the competitive side of male gender training, and those hierarchies determine value between men and over women. This hierarchical power system objectifies women in such a way that it makes violence against them more acceptable and likely.[23] In an interesting newspaper article from the *Seattle Times*, a lawyer is reported to have used the following argument to defend his client from being punished for the crime of sexual assault of which he had been found guilty. The lawyer said, "Hostility toward women, I think, is something that is culturally instilled in men. It's part of our culture that has been for hundreds of years, that violence against women is not unacceptable. Consequently, my client should not be punished for being culturally male."[24]

Ewing writes, "The ruling paradigm for male supremacy remains to this hour, physical violence."[25] And, it is often effective. McMahon and Pence have studied men who batter. They conclude, ". . . when asked, violent men are quite clear about what it can accomplish: 'she would listen' 'she would drop the order for protection' 'next time she'd think twice.' Such men benefit from their violence. How much more seductive are explanations that say a man's violence is an expression of his insecurity or impulsiveness."[26]

THE ROLE OF THE CHURCH IN RESISTING AND PREVENTING DOMESTIC VIOLENCE

When we look at how the culture sets up girls and boys, women and men to live in relationships of dominance and violence with each other, we begin to see how important it would be for the Church to provide counter-stories for girls and boys, women and men that would work against this kind of gender socialization that makes women and men vulnerable to violence in their intimate relationships. And, it would become apparent that the Church is a natural place to actively work against the kind of emotional and physical violence that occurs between men and women in marriages in a patriarchal culture. Yet, the Church, speaking generally, does not have a good track record in working with victims of family violence. Religious leaders tend to participate in the same silence and silencing of domestic abuse victims and their stories that the culture does. They have used theological justifications, particularly the sanctity of the family, to justify its silencing of domestic abuse victims. They have been in unquestioning collusion with patriarchy in terms of assuming the normativity (and believability) of males. And, they have not wanted to participate in the kind of upheaval that it would cause to actively advocate on behalf of victims, especially since it is often the perpetrators who have the power and authority within local churches.

Most studies that have been done about the usefulness of clergy in situations of domestic abuse find that they are rated as both the least used resource and the least helpful resource compared to family, friends, psychotherapists, family doctors, and social service agencies. In a recent study, researchers found that clergy effectiveness is consistently low, and they speculated that this was probably due to clergy endorsement of traditional teachings concerning the sanctity of marriage. In addition, a research group sent out a two-page questionnaire to 5700 pastors, and fewer than 10% of the questionnaires were returned. The researchers concluded that pastors lacked interest in or were hostile to the notion of domestic abuse. They also noted that the clergy who did return their questionnaires seemed to be concerned about battered women but indicated that they were torn by theological perspectives that seemed to be in conflict with the best interests of the women.[27] These are very serious issues if, indeed, clergy are feeling that they are not able to be helpful to victims of intimate violence, especially wife battering or spousal rape, because they are trapped by theological doctrine that mandates patriarchal power. Pastoral theology must commit itself to closing this gap between theological doctrine and the well-being of women, and pastors need to work through the theological ambiguity that they may carry regarding women and men and the dynamics of marriage. It is interesting that women who rated their pastors helpful tended to be from churches which normally addressed social problems in general and which created an environment where women felt safe in coming forward with their stories. They were also more likely to rate their pastors as helpful if they were willing to take action to intervene in the violence, not just to listen passively to them.[28]

PREMARITAL PREPARATION AS A STRATEGY OF RESISTANCE AGAINST DOMESTIC VIOLENCE

Where does this leave us in terms of premarital preparation and the planning of wedding services as sources of prevention and resistance against marital violence? It is important to recognize that premarital preparation has limits that are significant. Women and men who are approaching marriage are generally unwilling to explore issues or problems in their relationships. In a recent study, premarital couples were interviewed about what kind of premarital preparation they would find useful/not useful. In other words, what kind of program would encourage them to take advantage of the opportunity for premarital preparation and what kind of programs would they avoid. The most frequently identified non-useful premarital approach was being asked to disclose secrets or past relationship issues that might threaten the stability of the relationship. However, in that same study, couples strongly felt that the three most helpful elements in premarital preparation would be to improve communication, assist in problem-solving skills, and identify and modify behavioral patterns (especially strategies for changing problematic interactions). Given these hopes by couples approaching marriage, one could suggest that addressing issues of current or potential violence would be welcomed by premarital couples.[29]

Another recent study raised the concern that significant issues in relationships should not be raised in a context where guidance in addressing those issues would be unavailable or inadequate.[30] This means that if religious leaders are going to directly raise concerns about violence, they need to be well prepared to make appropriate referrals for further counseling work or be prepared to do this specialized counseling themselves.

A third issue to be considered in creating a premarital preparation program that addresses violence is the reality that there is no agreed upon or comprehensive theory of premarital preparation available to us. Premarital preparation, in large part, is idiosyncratic to the religious leaders doing it and, in fact, many religious leaders do not routinely do premarital preparation at all. According to the study cited above, 75% of first marriages occur in religious organizations, but fewer than one-half of those organizations currently provide premarital preparation services.[31] Yet, there is considerable evidence that thoughtful premarital preparation with an emphasis on skills and family exploration is useful in reducing the likelihood of divorce. There is no data on whether it is helpful in reducing violence although there is one study that suggests that the use of some inventories (in particular, PREP) may reduce the likelihood of relationship aggression.[32] We have a lot of research still to do on what makes an effective premarital preparation program as well as education for clergy and religious leaders in the importance of offering this service to couples approaching marriage. Although there are good resources now available in training religious leaders in premarital preparation, it is important for seminaries and continuing education programs to make sure those resources are made available and the importance of this program emphasized. It is one of the few times when both members of a couple are available to their pastor where in-depth conversation about their relationship is expected. This is an opportunity that should not be ignored, for skill-building in general and for screening of and resistance to marital violence. And, textbooks in premarital preparation need to include material on couple violence and how to address its likelihood. In a survey of the five most popular premarital preparation texts I found no mention of any strategies on how to screen for or work against intimate violence nor, indeed, any mention of the problem. Given the statistics named above and the prevalence of texts on how to care for battered women, this seems to be glaring absence in the literature.

WHAT CAN WE DO?

As named above, it is important for religious leaders to understand and accept the prevalence of the problem of domestic violence and that it exists in their congregations. And, it is crucial that their theological ambivalence about actively working against domestic violence be resolved. But what else can we do at a practical level once these issues are resolved?

I would suggest the following strategies in ministry toward the goal of screening for, reducing levels of, and resisting the potential for domestic violence.

Premarital Preparation

- First, we need to explore power arrangements in premarital couples. Stahmann and Hiebert, in their book *Premarital and Remarital Counseling*, suggest a technique called the Dynamic Relationship History. In that process, a couple is asked to articulate aspects to their relationship that indicate how they make decisions and, to a certain extent, how relationship power is arranged. This is a helpful starting point for looking at the potential of domestic violence. As we know, wife battering is more about control and dominance than it is about anger or conflict. Looking at patterns of power and decision-making can be helpful (and non-threatening) in exploring the potential for control and emotional/physical violence.
- Because wife battering is about control, premarital preparation inventories need to go beyond the issues of conflict resolution to explore these concerns of power and dominance.
- Religious leaders who are doing premarital preparation need to ask direct questions of couples about their family history of emotional and physical violence and how they make meaning out of those experiences. If there has been a family history of violence in the parents' (or even grandparents') marriages, it is important to ask the couple how that family history takes shape in their own lives. Where are they vulnerable to repeating patterns and how they might cope with history repeating itself.

- Religious leaders need to be willing to ask couples directly if they have had experiences of emotional or physical violence in their relationship and what the outcome of that experience was. If the religious leader suspects, for reasons of family history or because of direct observation of the couple, that emotional or physical violence may exist in this relationship, it would be important to meet with each member of the couple separately in order to ask each member about relationship dynamics and the possibility of relationship violence without them having to fear the reaction of the other partner to their answer. If the religious leader discovers violence in the relationship, it would be very important to do some educational work about the persistence of relationship violence once it occurs and the importance of counseling help for each member of the couple (not couple counseling). It is important to let them know that marriage will not change negative behaviors that are already apparent in the relationship. Men who are engaging in emotional or physical violence in their relationship need to move through very specific counseling processes (described elsewhere in this volume) to assist them in ending their strategies of violence and learning to hold themselves (and be held) accountable. Women need to address their tendencies to take responsibility for violence against them in intimate relationships and to take responsibility for not accepting dynamics of violence in themselves and their partners.
- Finally, most premarital inventories and proposed preparation approaches allow for diversity in role definitions in marriage. Given the discussion above regarding gender role socialization and vulnerability to the dynamics of violence, I would propose that a "complementarity" approach to gender roles is no longer acceptable. Couples need to be guided toward new images of male-female relationship that emphasize equal power, equal access to resources and to decision-making, and shared responsibilities. Both members of a couple need to be responsible for private roles like homemaking and parenting and for public roles like employment and political action. The notion of "headship" in a marriage (often supported by certain theological interpretations) needs to be replaced by the notion of authentic partnership. Although most couples will claim this commitment to equality, when details about decision-making, power dynamics, behavioral strategies during conflict, and so on, it becomes clear that power is not equally shared or claimed.

Wedding Rituals

- Weddings are full of symbolic actions that indicate the nature of the relationship, the kind of commitment the bride and groom are making to each other, and the way they are planning to move into the future together. It is important that the pastor and couple plan these symbolic elements of a wedding with a clear understanding of what they are saying to each other and the community about their relationship. The symbolic aspect of weddings are probably the most powerful in conveying the core meanings of the marriage, and it is important to take the issues of partnership, equality, and mutual empowerment seriously.

The vows that are spoken between the marrying couple also need to be carefully created to convey the intentions of the couple to live respectfully, mutually, and justly with each other.

- Religious leaders should be clear about the theological ambiguity of some of our religious traditions and should choose Scripture passages and homily themes in keeping with strategies of resistance against dominance, inequality, and violence.

Ongoing Ministry in the Church

- This leads to a larger issue in ministry and that is the need to find ways to shift the dynamics of gender socialization and gender-driven power arrangements as a central mission of the Church. If a congregation consistently lifts up issues of gender injustice in its blatant and subtle forms, it will be more likely that couples approaching marriage will already be addressing these issues that increase the likelihood of domestic violence. This is a major topic in its own right, beyond the scope of this article, but it seems to me that we need to address issues of gender justice consistently throughout the various ministries in the church. This is not as easy as it sounds. For example, one pastor that I know is deeply committed to issues of gender justice, uses inclusive language at every level of worship and education, and raises the accomplishments of women in his sermons and classes. Yet, the usual illustration for raising the accomplishments of women tends to praise women for stereotypical feminine traits, especially that of self-sacrifice which only supports problematic gender roles. These are subtle yet crucial awarenesses to gain in trying to find ways to resist patterns of dominance and violence in gender relations.

- Finally, I would urge pastors to raise issues of domestic violence directly in their sermons, newsletter columns, and adult education classes as a way to send a clear message that there is never an acceptable justification for intimate violence in families. There are resources now available to help religious leaders address these topics in sermons and liturgy that we need to learn how to use. Churches need to actively participate in generating theological counter-stories to the epidemic of violence and gender injustice in families today.

CONCLUSION

I have no idealized expectation that religious leaders learning how to raise the issues of domestic violence in premarital preparation will end this epidemic. However, it is one more piece of the puzzle in which we need to be actively involved as we seek to participate in God's vision for increasing love and justice in our world. And, at this point in time, it is a missing puzzle piece in our pastoral ministries.

NOTES

1. For example, the United Methodist *Book of Worship* suggests that the individual candles remain lit after the Unity candle has been lit for symbolic reasons.

2. Parts of this article appeared in a chapter entitled "Narratives of Harm" in Jeanne Stevenson Moessner (ed.) *In Her Own Time* (Abingdon, 2000).

3. Donaldson, Lufkin and Jenrette Newsletter, May 3, 1996. p 13.

4. Margi Laud McCue. *Domestic Violence: A Reference Handbook* (Santa Barbara: ABC-CL10, 1995) 81.

5. McCue, 79.

6. Lyn Mikel Brown and Carol Gilligan, *Meeting at the Crossroads: Women's Psychology and Girls' Development* (Cambridge: Harvard University Press, 1992) 216.

7. Robert Levant and William Pollack, "Introduction." In *A New Psychology of Men*, ed. Ronald Levant and William Pollack (New York: Basic Books, 1995) 1.

8. James O'Neil, Glenn Good, and Sarah Holmes, "Fifteen Years of Theory and Research on Men's Gender Role Conflict: New Paradigms for Empirical Research." In *A New Psychology of Men*, ed. Ronald Levant and William Pollack (New York: Basic Books, 1995) 171.

9. O'Neil, Good, and Holmes, 188-191.

10. Richard Eisler, "The Relationship between Masculine Gender Role Stress and Men's Health Risk: The Validation of A Construct." In *A New Psychology of Men*, ed. Ronald Levant and William Pollack (New York: Basic Books, 1995) 207-225.

11. Gary Brooks and Louise Silverstein, "Understanding the Dark Side of Masculinity: An Interactive Systems Model," In *A New Psychology of Men*, ed. Ronald Levant and William Pollack (New York: Basic Books, 1995) 284.

12. Michael Cascardi and Daniel O'Leary, "Depressive Symptomatology, Self-esteem, and Self-blame in Battered Women." *Journal of Family Violence*, (17 #4 1992) 255.

13. Lora Bex Lempert, "A Narrative Analysis of Abuse: Connecting the Personal, the Rhetorical, and the Structural." *Journal of Contemporary Ethnography* (22 #4 January, 1994) 428.

14. Piera Serra, "Physical Violence in the Couple Relationship: A Contribution toward the Analysis of the Context. *Family Process* (32 #1 (March, 1993) 25.

15. Lempert, 432.

16. Serra, 29.

17. Carol Ember and Melvin Ember, "War, Socialization, and Interpersonal Violence." *Journal of Conflict Resolution*, (38 #4 December, 1994) 633.

18. Paul Yelsma, "Affective Orientations of Perpetrators, Victims, and Functional Spouses. *Journal of Interpersonal Violence*, (11 #2 June, 1996) 141-161.

19. Wayne Ewing, "The Civic Advocacy of Men's Violence." In *A New Psychology of Men*, ed. Ronald Levant and William Pollack (New York: Basic Books, 1995).

20. Wayne Ewing, 304.

21. Wayne Ewing, 304.

22. Michael Kaufman, "The Construction of Masculinity and the Triad of Men's Violence." In *Men's Lives*, 3rd Edition, ed. Michael Kimmel and Michael Messner (Boston: Allyn and Bacon, 1995) 17.

23. Joseph Pleck, "Men's Power with Women, Other Men, and Society: A Men's Movement Analysis." In *Men's Lives*, 3rd Edition, ed. Michael Kimmel and Michael Messner (Boston: Allyn and Bacon, 1995) 5-12.

24. Marie Fortune and James Poling, "Calling to Accountability: The Church's Response to Abusers," in *Violence Against Women and Children* ed. by Carol Adams and Marie Fortune (New York: Continuum Press, 1995) 454.

25. Wayne Ewing, 301.

26. Martha McMahon and Ellen Pence. "Replying to Daniel O'Leary." *Journal of Interpersonal Violence* (September, 1996) 452-55.

27. Alberta Wood and Maureen McHugh. "Woman Battering: The Response of Clergy." *Pastoral Psychology* (42, 3 1994) 191.

28. Wood and McHugh (1994) 192.

29. Carolos Valiente, Catherine Belanger, and Ana Estrada. "Helpful and Harmful Expectations of Premarital Interventions." *Journal of Sex and Marital Therapy* (28, 2002) 71.

30. Scott Stanley, Howard Markman, Lydia Olmos-Gall, P. Antonio et al. "Community-based Premarital Prevention: Clergy and LayLeaders on the Front Lines." *Family Relations*, (50, 1, 2001) 76.

31. Scott Stanley et al. (2001) 67.

32. Scott Stanley. "Making a Case for Premarital Education." *Family Relations*, (50, 3, 2001) 274.

Moving from Vulnerability
to Empowerment

Ted Stoneberg

SUMMARY. In this article, the author explores the literature about male identity formation, especially in adolescence, and suggests religious and psychological resources for healing that can lead to nonviolence. He argues that male violence is motivated most deeply by fear of vulnerability and pain that is present for many men but not addressed by traditional stereotypes of masculinity. Finding safe places to explore this vulnerability can lead to healing and empowerment so that men can be mentors to other men in their own healing. *[Article copies available for a fee from The Haworth Document Delivery Service: 1-800-HAWORTH. E-mail address: <docdelivery@haworthpress.com> Website: <http://www.HaworthPress.com> © 2002 by The Haworth Press, Inc. All rights reserved.]*

KEYWORDS. Male identity formation, adolescent formation, male violence

"The violent man, the lawbreaker. Why do we wait so late to see these men's desperation? Many of them can be spotted as children in elementary school."[1] These are the passionate words of Gus Napier during a plenary presentation at the annual convention of the American

[Haworth co-indexing entry note]: "Moving from Vulnerability to Empowerment." Stoneberg, Ted. Co-published simultaneously in *Journal of Religion & Abuse* (The Haworth Pastoral Press, an imprint of The Haworth Press, Inc.) Vol. 4, No. 3, 2002, pp. 61-73; and: *Men's Work in Preventing Violence Against Women* (ed: James Newton Poling, and Christie Cozad Neuger) The Haworth Pastoral Press, an imprint of The Haworth Press, Inc., 2002, pp. 61-73. Single or multiple copies of this article are available for a fee from The Haworth Document Delivery Service [1-800-HAWORTH, 9:00 a.m. - 5:00 p.m. (EST). E-mail address: docdelivery@haworthpress.com].

Association for Marriage and Family Therapy in 1989. Similarly James Garbarino in *Lost Boys* cites the research of Leonard Eron and colleagues. In the 1960s these researchers asked eight-year-olds

> . . . to identify the aggressive children in their classrooms. . . . When they followed up on these children three decades later, they found that, by and large, the children who had been identified as aggressive at age eight became adults who at age thirty-eight hit family members, get into fights in the community, and drive their cars aggressively.[2]

It seems apparent that if we want to have a society in which men are neither abusive and violent toward women in particular nor toward children and other men, we need to begin the correction with the way we raise boys. We must also shape a post-patriarchal image of masculinity. Although there are many ways for men and women to cooperate toward achieving this goal, it would appear that the starting place needs to be with us men. We must acknowledge our disconnection from each other, from our sons and other boys in the community, and especially from ourselves.

The women's movements generated energy from the awareness of the pain that came from being oppressed and defined by men. It has taken some of the women socialized under the patriarchal perspective longer than others to become aware of their hurt and need for change, but a significant number rather quickly helped each other raise their consciousness and together shaped their own definitions of themselves as empowered persons.

IDENTIFYING VULNERABILITY IN THE OPPRESSOR

We who have held societal and political power through the years are much slower to become aware of how patriarchal images of masculinity have also injured and hurt us and our descendents.[3] Ironically the patriarchal image is one that socializes men to deny any vulnerability or hurt, i.e., to keep a tough exterior to avoid facing the interior potential for woundedness. It is no wonder that men are so slow to be aware of the losses and pain in our lives or to acknowledge that violence against women is not in men's best interests. William Pollack in *Real Boys* writes:

> I believe that boys, feeling ashamed of their vulnerability, mask their emotions and ultimately their true selves. This unnecessary

disconnection–from family and then from self–causes many boys to feel alone, helpless, and fearful. And yet society's prevailing myths about boys do not leave room for such emotions, and so the boy feels he is not measuring up. . . . And so a boy has been "hardened," just as society thinks he should be.[4]

This masculine straitjacket is the social expectation that we take on as young boys and is generally part of our whole lives unless we are among the minority of men who are not raised to take on these restrictive assumptions. It is only when we experience a major grief that we become aware of our vulnerability. Generally men do not seek out psychotherapy or other forms of help unless they have experienced or feel the threat of a significant loss. Perhaps it will take the demise of Euro-American men's near-total social control of others before there will be enough pain to bring about changes in their views of masculinity.

Significant factors in the masculine straitjacket are a lack of emotional literacy and empathy toward others. Kindlon and Thompson and Garbarino all point to the work of Dan Goleman on "emotional intelligence." Garbarino finds that violent boys suffer from a kind of "emotional retardation."[5] Kindlon and Thompson write:

> In our experience with families, we find that most girls get lots of encouragement from an early age to be emotionally literate–to be reflective and expressive of their own feelings and to be responsive to the feelings of others. Many boys do not receive this kind of encouragement, and their emotional illiteracy shows, at a young age, when they act with careless disregard for the feelings of others at home, at school, or on the playground.[6]

It is not surprising that we find this same issue in adult men, and it is particularly a problem in violent and abusive men. When one is aware of his/her feelings, there is the option of verbal expression which improves impulse control. When this is absent, it is not surprising that such persons resort to expression through movement or action. It clearly reduces the alternatives that a person entertains. Learning to express one's feelings rather than act on them is usually a key element in anger management training.

William Pollack writes,

> When I counsel couples, I am often struck by the fact that many of the skills required to succeed in adult relationships are those we resist teaching to growing boys–skills of connection (empathy, negotiation, and compromise), instead of competitiveness; the ability to be dependent and vulnerable and to share one's troubles, instead of the ability to keep a stiff upper lip and handle pain alone.[7]

One of the major vulnerabilities that boys and men seek to avoid is the feeling of shame. It is particularly difficult and mostly impossible to share our shame with other men because the normal "rules" in men's relationships are either to make light of the vulnerability or to intensify it by teasing and harassing the one who is in shame. The one "acceptable" emotion for men in the masculine straitjacket is anger. Anger becomes the funnel emotion in place of sadness, guilt, shame, fear, grief, and even love. The primary function of the anger is to protect against vulnerability.

The sense of shame in boys may have many sources but chief among them is the harsh discipline that is imposed on boys "to make men out of them." But interestingly, grown men in therapy will say that if it had not been for the harsh discipline that they received frequently from their fathers, they would have ended up in much more trouble. These men do not seem to be even remotely aware of what the stringent discipline cost them or how it drove them into isolation with their shame. What the harsh discipline does is to short-circuit the process of helping a boy reflect upon the effects of his behavior and consider alternative ways of behaving. Instead he is left with a mark of shame which he is likely either to use to turn against himself or to turn against others in the form of violence.

UNTOLD, UNDERLYING PAIN

Most adult men enjoy telling stories about their childhood friendships and activities but do not readily share stories of boy to boy cruelty. Kindlon and Thompson refer to this as a culture of cruelty in which boys learn to tease and bully one another, particularly if a boy dares to show vulnerability. There are many painful experiences of domination, betrayal, humiliation, and fear that remain hidden in silence. The patriarchal masculinity calls for silence and bravado rather than admission of vulnerability. The silence of boys and men regarding their victimhood from others leaves the impression that they are "cool" and have no problems or pain.

The silence practiced around this cruelty promotes boys growing into men who seek to have social control over others, particularly over women and others they perceive to be vulnerable, including other men. This is reinforced and supported by most other men around who do not question or challenge this control. It seems unimaginable that a group of men, frequently athletes, will together participate in the gang rape of a woman. One would expect that the group would prevent the first perpetrator from doing the deed. Unfortunately they were all groomed through their culture of cruelty to seek to have power over others and to join those who exercise power over others so that they will not be seen as being "soft." A first step in men stopping violence toward women will need to be men breaking through their own denial regarding the violence they themselves have experienced from these same socially controlling mennorms.

Bill Moyer interviewed a group of African American men in a recovery group. The video is simply called "The Circle of Recovery."[8] These men finally found a safe place to be vulnerable with other men. The viewer is aware that this is a group for recovering addicts but is left with the clear awareness that the main recovery for these men was no longer having to be silent about their inner pain and hurts. In this safe setting they could be vulnerable and feel connected, and yet still confront and challenge each other.

There are other stories of adult men today gathering in accountability groups that work at attaining this level of connectedness with each other. But the struggle is slow going and often not sustained because of this deeply embedded "culture of cruelty" that often makes friendships between men shallow and transitory. If we men can learn to gather together in such groups where it is safe to be vulnerable with each other, we could go a long way toward decreasing the abuse and violence of men toward others. An accountability group of men can serve as a container for their anger and rage. It is helpful for men to be able to vocalize these feelings in the presence of other men who are not intimidated or overwhelmed by the intensity of the expression. Then the group members need to challenge each other to channel that energy toward constructive purposes.

Unfortunately there are far too many examples of men gathering in groups to fuel their hate and rage. Sometimes they even plot together on how to act on that hate. It is no wonder that women have fears about men gathering together. They have seen the results far too often. Accountability groups, however, are not large gatherings. They are simply safe places to be vulnerable. These gatherings consist typically from two to eight men meeting regularly with each other. James Nelson realized how much he wanted improved male to male relationships when he experienced physical and emotional closeness with his father as the man was dying. When he returned to his home, he called six other men and told them that he needed them closer in his life.[9] At a professional gathering about three years ago Nelson shared that he has met with this group of men continuously now for almost 20 years.

When Al Gore experienced the fear of losing his son, he became motivated to seek out a prayer group. He said in an interview with Richard Louv that "a man without a group of friends to whom he can turn is an accident waiting to happen."[10] Adult men can be immensely helpful to adolescent and young boys by openly sharing their own experiences of vulnerability and by giving boys windows into their own souls. Otherwise all these boys know and hear are the stories of heroics and toughness. Boys need models showing them that vulnerability is not unmanly.

James Nelson quotes Joy M. K. Bussert, who says, "After listening to the stories of countless women in shelters, and after sitting in on several treatment groups for violent men, I can only conclude that battering–at least in part–is a substitute for tears."[11] Unfortunately, living with the patriarchal image of masculinity means learning not to cry if one is to be considered manly. Thus at an early age we men learn not to own or show our vulnerability. Instead, we as boys are socialized by both men and women to control our emotions and present a picture of being in control. When we learn to do this well, is it any wonder that we seek to control those around us and our environment?

Post-patriarchal socialization of men needs to help boys and men stay aware of and express their vulnerability with each other, especially with other men. Along with this awareness, the new masculine image needs to replace "power over" others with "power with" others.

THROUGH DESPAIR TO EMPOWERMENT

During the nuclear freeze movement days Joanna Macy conducted "Despair and Empowerment Workshops." She helped those of us who participated to truly despair our vulnerability to a nuclear holocaust. It was only after we had fully experienced and worked with our despair that she encouraged us to be aware of our empowerment. In the same way, instead of being paralyzed and confused about how to be a "man" today, it is time for men to despair the brokenness of our masculine images. Then, only after serious despair work is done, we can consider where empowerment might begin to take place in the forming of a new masculinity.

In the current scandal within the Roman Catholic Church regarding the disclosures of priests sexually abusing boys, there is the potential for bringing about the necessary despair over the destructiveness of power when it is used over the less powered person. The public exposure of this crisis could bring into the open the hidden pain of men who have been abused in childhood. Ironically it may take this acknowledgement to provoke also despair about the violence of men against women. It will take something of this magnitude to break through the denial system of men regarding this issue.

This is certainly in keeping with the Christian story of life coming out of death, but the death needs to take place before new life can come forth. Hanging on to the old images and attempting to revive them will not work. Patriarchal images need to die so that new life can come forth in men. This will be hard work and will surely involve despair and grieving.

LEARNING EMPATHY FOR OTHERS

In addition to limited or no awareness of their vulnerability, men also have poor training for being empathetic toward others. Kindlon and Thompson state that "studies of parent interactions with both boys and girls suggest that when a girl asks a question about emotions, her mother will give longer explanations. She's more likely to speculate with her daughter about the reasons behind the emotion or to validate or amplify her daughter's observation. . . ."[12] Empathy is clearly part of a girl's socialization, but it seems that we generally do not expect or encourage boys to practice this "feeling with" another person. It is clear that in the bullying and teasing that boys do with each other, empathy is not in operation.

Men and women can join each other in the project of teaching boys to practice empathy toward others. When fathers model empathy in their interactions with others and with their sons, it has a profound effect on their offspring. Mothers also are in a position through their parenting to encourage and reinforce empathy in their sons as well as their daughters. If boys are not taught to understand other people's feelings, then they are not only unable to be empathetic, but they are likely to misread the cues they receive from others.

Intimacy in a relationship with a woman requires sensitivity, respect, and tenderness, and these are precisely the characteristics that men and boys who take on the "masculine straitjacket" are taught to see as feminine characteristics to be avoided. Instead, the culture of cruelty teaches men to trust power, dominance and denial, attributes which are contrary to promoting intimacy. Girls and women can represent the vulnerable, alien qualities and thus become the enemies because they have the power to inflict the most humiliating emotional hurt. Therefore, they must be dominated so that they cannot inflict their pain.[13]

> Voices of Love and Freedom is a program developed by Patrick Walker . . . and Robert Selman . . . The intent of the program is to help kids learn how to resolve conflicts without resorting to violence. The program uses storytelling to provoke the participants into discussing the characters and events and making connections to their own lives. The idea is to help kids see actions and situations from the perspectives of the different characters, and to understand that we can all feel vulnerable and threatened, and that we all have a shared humanity . . . This kind of perspective-taking makes it more likely that a boy will feel empathy for others' weaknesses and concerns, and less shame about his own.[14]

It is quite clear that the new myth and image of masculinity needs to open us men to accept and be aware of our own vulnerability and to value and practice empathy for others, particularly when others are vulnerable or open toward us. For Christian men, the life of Jesus certainly presents an effective model of a man who was aware of his vulnerability. He knew what he faced as he entered Jerusalem. He showed empathy in his words from the cross and in his ministry for those who were neglected, oppressed, and forgotten by the majority of the society. Jesus also attempts to heal the "wounded image" of God by portraying God as compassionate and caring. For example, God is likened to the father of the Prodigal son who runs to meet and welcome his wayward son. God is no longer the one so distant and so removed that even his God's name cannot be named. Rather God can be addressed and called upon as someone very near and accessible. This is particularly remarkable in light of the patriarchal society in which Jesus lived and in light of the then-prevalent patriarchal imagery of God.

Jesus also encourages us, particularly men, to move from vulnerability to empowerment when he says that if we want to be his disciples we must die to our centering on ourselves and our pride. We must lose ourselves in God so that we will be empowered with a new life (Mark 8:34-36; Matt. 16:24-26). This particular passage could be very helpful for men who seek to control and dominate others and who are centered on themselves.

FATHERS TURNING THEIR HEARTS TOWARD THE CHILDREN

The Hebrew canon in Protestant Bibles ends with these verses: "But before the great and terrible day of the Lord comes, I will send you the prophet Elijah. He will bring fathers and children together again; otherwise, I would have come and destroyed your country" (Malachi 4:5,6-TEV). The image of God's shalom is that fathers' hearts will be turned toward their children. The prophecy assumes that fathers have been separated or alienated from their children and that reconciliation is needed. Essentially these same words occur again when the angel addresses Zechariah during his service in the temple and announces the coming birth of a son with these words: "He will go before him as forerunner, possessed by the spirit and power of Elijah, to reconcile father and child, to convert the rebellious to the ways of the righteous, to prepare a people that shall be fit for the Lord" (Luke 1:17-NEB). This prophecy points to an important reality, namely that when fathers and children are out of meaningful and wholesome contact with each other, destructiveness in the social order results.

Men's social control of women is often generated by displaced anger towards fathers who were physically or emotionally absent when, as boys, they were differentiating themselves from their mothers in order to develop their male identity. Without having emotional closeness with their fathers as they are appropriately pushing away and being pushed away from their mothers, boys learn to depend upon an "over-againstness" toward their mothers as necessary for the formation of their masculinity. Beneath this opposition toward women is a father-wounded son. In marital therapy I have seen how men who are very controlling of their wives begin to identify their own pain and hurt only when we explore together their relationship with their fathers. Once they name their own hurt, these men are more open to see how their controlling nature towards their wives is hurtful.

It has been shown in several studies that children who have fathers caringly involved in their lives grow up to be more socially competent, to have more compassion for others, to be more self-directed, and to be more persistent at solving problems.[15] Conversely, there is a high correlation between absent fathers and sons who later engage in drugs and delinquent behavior.

Kindlon and Thompson write:

> It is clear to us that the most emotionally resourceful and resilient boys are those whose fathers are part of the emotional fabric of the family, whose fathers care for them and show it in comforting, consistent ways. Sadly, it is a minority of fathers who share this kind of relationship with their sons.[16]

The problem is that many men are burdened with unresolved issues with their own fathers. The hearts of fathers have been turned away from the children for many generations. It is difficult to break this cycle and to replace it with active involvement in the lives of our own children. But our sons will be helped significantly if they observe us being emotionally honest about our own lives and if, in our responses to them, we give them permission to express their emotional vulnerability.

Research confirms what adolescent boys report about life with their fathers as being significant sources of conflict: competition, criticism, and lack of understanding.[17] Fathers tend not to simply listen to their sons but instead to relate to them as disciplinarians, leaders/teachers or boosters. This means that the adolescent son gets significant doses of his father's temperament and little of the care and respect he longs to receive. This also means that adolescent boys are least likely to confide their true feelings and conflicts with their fathers.

> Patterns of emotional isolation can change. Fathers can change them. A man who wants a more satisfying relationship with his son can begin to build it in simple but meaningful ways: a bedtime story, a game of catch, a compliment, a smile. The willingness to try is, itself, the start of a new pattern that can replace the disappointment of emotional distance with a legacy of love.[18]

The National Center for Fathering (10200 W. 75th Street, Suite 267, Shawnee Mission, KA 66204) directed by Ken Canfield does one-day fathering conferences around the country and encourages after conference support groups for fathers. This program seeks to be the leading research and resource development center which equips men in their fathering role. It has been affiliated with Promise Keepers and promotes an Evangelical Christian perspective.

The National Fatherhood Initiative (101 Lake Forest Blvd., Suite 360, Gaithersburg, MD 20877) is attempting to be a society-wide movement to confront the problem of father absence. Local communities can be affiliated with this Initiative and receive resources. They have sponsored several significant TV spot advertisements to sensitize men to this issue.

Gordon Dalbey, another Evangelical Christian, has written material and conducted retreats and other conferences to help men heal their masculine souls. He has a website (*http://www.abbafather.com/*) on which he regularly communicates where he is doing retreats and what he is writing. This has become a full-time ministry for him.

There are a few other programs which can be found on an Internet search that are seeking to address this issue, but the above listed ones are those familiar to me. In local communities there may be several attempts to address the concern of developing boys into more dependable and empathetic men who seek to share power with others. In my own community there are two examples of this kind of work. One is called Prime Time for Youth and is focused on mentoring boys in later elementary school who are at risk. The other group was formed by a retired assistant superintendent of our public school. He gets a few other adult men to help him mentor third grade boys for several weeks. Both of these programs are led by African American men and are focused primarily on serving African American boys.

Adult men who have been nurtured and loved by their fathers will be empowered to have empathy and concern for others. These are men who get their sense of masculinity from being personally strengthened rather than seeking their masculinity from their control over women.

> In *The Prince* Machiavelli wrote that "the question arises whether it is better to be loved rather than feared, or feared rather than loved. It might perhaps be answered that we should wish to be both: but since love and fear can hardly exist together, if we must choose between them, it is far safer to be feared than loved."[19]

But is this really true today? Who is safer when men are feared rather than loved? No one is safer, not even the man who may be socialized to think it is best not ever to be vulnerable. Rather, the truly empowered man seeks to be loved and to show concern and caring to others. His goal is to engender genuine love, which ultimately is far safer than fear.

NOTES

1. Augustus Napier, "Growing Up Married: Men and Commitment." Audiotape of a plenary session at the 1989 AAMFT Annual Convention.

2. James Garbarino, *Lost Boys: Why Our Sons Turn Violent and How We Can Save Them,* New York: Anchor Books, 1999, page 66.

3. This article is written from the author's own social location as a white male and does not include the significantly different issues for ethnic and racial minority persons regarding vulnerability and empowerment.

4. William Pollack, *Real Boys: Rescuing Our Sons from the Myths of Boyhood,* New York: Henry Holt and Company, 1998, page XXIV.

5. Garbarino, op. cit., page 53.

6. Dan Kindlon and Michael Thompson, *Raising Cain: Protecting the Emotional Life of Boys,* New York: Ballantine Books, 1999, page 5.

7. Pollack, op. cit., page 98.

8. Bill Moyers, "Circle of Recovery" Mystic Fire Video, 1991.

9. James B. Nelson, *Between Two Gardens: Reflections on Sexuality and Religious Experience,* New York: The Pilgrim Press, 1983, page 45.

10. Richard Louv, "Al Gore on Fatherhood," *Parents,* February, Vol. 70, no. 2:47.

11. James B. Nelson, *The Intimate Connection: Male Sexuality, Masculine Spirituality,* Philadelphia: The Westminster Press, page 71.

12. Kindlon and Thompson, op. cit., page 17.

13. Ibid., page 210.

14. Pollack, op. cit., pages 355-356.

15. Correlational findings should not be understood as showing causality. Therefore, it is important to say here that there are many children raised by single mothers or in female households who also develop these positive traits. The purpose of mentioning the studies is only to emphasize that fathers can have a significant influence on their children when they are actively involved in parenting.

16. Kindlon and Thompson, op. cit., page 96.

17. Ibid., page 103.

18. Ibid., page 114.

19. Frank Pittman, *Man Enough: Fathers, Sons, and the Search for Masculinity,* New York: P. Putnam's Sons, 1993, page 93.

BIBLIOGRAPHY

Dalbey, Gordon, 1988, *Healing the Masculine Soul.* Dallas: Word Publishing.

Garbarino, James, 1999, *Lost Boys: Why Our Sons Turn Violent and How We Can Save Them.* New York: Anchor Books.

Kindlon, Dan and Michael Thompson, 1999, *Raising Cain: Protecting the Emotional Life of Boys.* New York: Ballatine Books.

Moyers, Bill, 1991, "Circle of Recovery." New York: Mystic Fire Video.

Nelson, James, 1983, *Between Two Gardens: Reflections on Sexuality and Religious Experience.* New York: The Pilgrim Press.

_____, 1988, *The Intimate Connection: Male Sexuality, Masculine Spirituality*. Philadelphia: The Westminster Press.

Napier, Augustus, 1988, "Growing Up Married: Men and Commitment." Audiotape of a plenary presentation at the 1989 AAMFT Annual Convention.

Pittman, Frank, 1993, *Man Enough: Fathers, Sons, and the Search for Masculinity*. New York: G.P. Putnam's Sons.

Pollack, William, 1998, *Real Boys: Rescuing Our Sons from the Myths of Boyhood*. New York: Henry Holt and Company.

The Dynamics of Power in Pastoral Care

Larry Kent Graham

SUMMARY. In this article, a male theologian struggles with images of God and power, arguing that the separative self and unilateral power of traditional theology is inadequate for men who are trying to confront their own violence. In contrast, he suggests the images of connective power, soluble selfhood, and living human web that can help men overcome their patriarchal formation and see women as partners in the religious journey. *[Article copies available for a fee from The Haworth Document Delivery Service: 1-800-HAWORTH. E-mail address: <docdelivery@haworthpress.com> Website: <http://www.HaworthPress.com> © 2002 by The Haworth Press, Inc. All rights reserved.]*

KEYWORDS. Sexual and domestic violence, images of God, self, power, web

INTRODUCTION

This article begins with a story that I heard sometime back from[1] Professor George Forell of the University of Iowa Religion Department. The story leads directly into the theme of this article: the dynamics of power in religious-based, or pastoral, care. Sometime during the later middle ages, when the Catholic Church was pressuring the Jewish

---

[Haworth co-indexing entry note]: "The Dynamics of Power in Pastoral Care." Graham, Larry Kent. Co-published simultaneously in *Journal of Religion & Abuse* (The Haworth Pastoral Press, an imprint of The Haworth Press, Inc.) Vol. 4, No. 3, 2002, pp. 75-88; and: *Men's Work in Preventing Violence Against Women* (ed: James Newton Poling, and Christie Cozad Neuger) The Haworth Pastoral Press, an imprint of The Haworth Press, Inc., 2002, pp. 75-88. Single or multiple copies of this article are available for a fee from The Haworth Document Delivery Service [1-800-HAWORTH, 9:00 a.m. - 5:00 p.m. (EST). E-mail address: docdelivery@haworthpress.com].

10.1300/J154v4n03_07

Community, the head Rabbi of the Jewish community in Rome gained an audience with the Pope to discuss his concerns and to try to bring understanding and tolerance. These wise men decided that too many words had been spoken, so they agreed to nonverbal, symbolic communication. The Pope began. He pointed his finger in the air, reached out his hand, and drew a large circle. The Rabbi responded by pointing his finger and extending his arm toward the Pope. Then the Pope held up two swords. The Rabbi pointed two fingers into the air, and extended them toward the Pope. Then the Pope held up an apple. The Rabbi held up a piece of flatbread. Both smiled warmly at one another and left with their attendants.

Afterwards, the Pope was asked what had happened. He said, "The meeting went very well. We have reached a common understanding. I began by drawing a circle to say, 'There is one universal church.' The Rabbi pointed at me and said, 'Yes, and you are the head of it!' I then held up two swords to say, 'There is a temporal and a spiritual realm.' The Rabbi pointed two fingers at me and said, 'Yes, and you are the head of both!' Then I held up an apple by which to say, 'Some people think that the world is round.' He held up a piece of matzoth to say, 'But we know that it is flat.' Our conversation has led to new understanding."

In the meantime, the Rabbi's associates were very concerned to learn what had transpired. The Rabbi too was pleased. He said, "The Pope began by drawing a large circle, saying, 'We have got you surrounded.' I responded by saying, 'But we can get to you, too!' He then held up two fingers to say we can cut you to pieces and hack you to bits! I said, 'But, I can poke out both of your eyes!' Then he took out his lunch, and I took out mine!"

The underlying point of the article is that we all have symbols and concepts about reality that found and sustain our sense of place in the world, and tie us to the social order. One central point of the story is that to be real, to thrive and to interrelate, requires an intact sense of power. It is precisely when that sense of power is threatened, diminished, or subordinated to the power of others, that symptomatic behavior has its genesis. Already, in the humor of the story, we discern how delusion and misapprehension by both leaders mask the true situation with respect to power. This communicative action relieved the tension, but preserved the status quo, without leading to deeper understandings and collaboratively shared power between the two leaders and their communities. Power remained unstable, dangerous, and the situation was still precarious.

The story evokes a longing for deeper communication, for genuine appreciation and understanding between these religious leaders and their communities. Where is the power necessary for this to occur? What extant power arrangements needed to change so that truth might replace misapprehension and delusion? Would something like 'care for the Other' have any bearing? Upon what foundation or interpretation of power might such care rest? How might it be activated? What might be its consequences?

In the remainder of this article I would like to explore how power is a central issue at all points in pastoral care. Power, as I am using the term, is a necessary capacity of any person or entity for it to be real. Power is therefore a core dimension of life. It is related to influence. Power is the capacity to influence another as an agent, and to be influenced by others as a receptor. Power is di-polar, characterized by agency as receptivity, pervasive, and capable of countless configurations. The controlling idea of this article is that pastoral care, grounded in the equalizing power of God's acceptance and liberative action, seeks to unmask destructive power arrangements and to change power dynamics in such a manner that participants in care become agents and receptors of relational justice. By relational justice, I mean, "The conditions by which everyone can be on mutually beneficial terms with one another, and with the natural order."

THE EMERGENCE OF POWER
AS A PROBLEM TO PASTORAL CARE

Experientially, power becomes a pastoral problem when someone does not have enough agency to prevent, endure, or overcome bad things happening to them or to their communities. They are too much the receptors of the agential power of others. The *locus classicus* of this problem is reflected in the question, "Why did God let this happen to me?" Or, "Why did God cause this?" The sufferer attributes his or her diminished power to the invasive or passive operation of divine agential power. Pastoral care practice cannot escape the conceptual and existential dilemmas arising from the formulations of divine and human power existing in the Western Christian tradition. I shall not focus on that axis of the question in this lecture. However, it must be noted that the classic formulation of unilateral, hierarchical power in much of the Christian tradition stands behind and legitimizes many of the forms of social power that I am going to discuss more fully.

The second place where issues of power emerge in pastoral care is when someone abuses another, or when social oppression is unmasked. In North America there is considerable attention given to these problems through some of the leading writers in the field of pastoral theology and care.[2] As Bonnie Miller McLemore, in her perceptive overview of the field, has said, pastoral care is moving from exclusive attention to "the living human document, to the living human web."[3] In such a move, issues of social power and justice become central to the task of care, rather than peripheral. James Poling's work on the abuse of power, and the evils of classism, racism, and sexism are some of the clearest examples. Kathleen Greider's book on re-thinking aggression in pastoral care is another. The abuse of power in large social structures is increasingly linked to the specific symptomatic circumstances that lead persons to pastoral care. Rearranging power becomes a central pastoral care skill, both diagnostically and strategically.

Let me recount a pastoral situation that will make what I am getting at more concrete. This "case" is used with permission, and only slightly modified.[4] While there are many issues in this case, I will emphasize those most pertinent to power dynamics. The caregiver is a Roman Catholic woman, who is a part of a lay ministry team of her local suburban parish. Her name is Kathy. She is about forty-five years of age. She has been assigned as a lay religious worker to a local shelter for women and children suffering from sexual and domestic violence. A director of the center called to ask her "to talk to a young woman about God, as she was fearful God would not forgive her for leaving her husband."

To Kathy, "this was a challenge and I wanted to help this woman see God as not being a cruel God. However, I did not want to force my feelings on her." Before the visit, she learned that the woman's name was Anna and that she had filed assault and battery charges against her alcoholic husband. "Arriving at the shelter, I saw this thin woman smoking a cigarette and holding tightly onto her son (who was around a year old). She seemed to be in her middle twenties and quite nervous. She was bruised around the eyes."

What follows is a verbatim of the pastoral interview that took place.

K. Hello, I'm Kathy. I've heard you've had quite a bad time.
A. Why does my husband beat me? One time he loved me. I had to leave. I am so afraid of him and what he will do to our son. I left while he was away from the house. I'm still afraid. (Rapidly smok-

ing her cigarette.) I pray God to forgive me for leaving him. He wants to take Frankie away from me. He says I'm no good.

K. Anna, this must have been hard for you to leave your home. However, it is a first step for you. You made a choice.

A. Yes. It was hard because I never made decisions. My husband always told me what to do and I did it. This last beating was too much. He gets violent when he drinks. I heard of this place and I called them.

K. Do your parents or friends know where you are?

A. No. I could not tell them. I was too embarrassed. My husband seemed always to enjoy embarrassing me in front of our friends. My parents live in Texas. I was brought up as a strict Catholic and my parents would be shocked.

K. Has it ever been easy for you to talk with your parish priest?

A. When reading the Bible it says the husband is head of the household. A wife should always be obedient to her husband. My husband, Bob, throws this up to me often. One time I thought about seeing our pastor. I decided not to because he probably would say the same thing.

K. Anna, how do you feel about yourself now? About your decision to come here and seek help?

A. I feel for the first time a sense of relief. Like I can breathe and I could not at home. I do not fear Frankie being hurt. We've been here now for three days. One thing, what if I decide to go back to him?

K. You are a different person because you made a choice by yourself. You have told someone outside and you have an easy reach for help. This is something you did not have before. This is in your favor. Even if you go back to him you are not the same as you were before. Only you can make a choice for yourself.

A. Do you think God hates me?

K. Why should God be angry with you? One person is not to abuse another. I believe God works through us and maybe this is a way of getting help for your husband.

A. I like talking with you. The others here look down on me. You look at me.

B. Thank you, Anna. Before I leave I would like to thank God for being with you. You'd be surprised at the strength you get from this little prayer.

Kathy does not record the prayer in her write up.

What about power in this situation? The pastoral situation has its occasion in a particular violent act within a history of regular and increasing family violence. Until she sought help, triggered by a need to use her power to protect her son, Anna was a rather helpless receptor, or victim, of her husband's agential power used violently to subordinate and control her. There is a huge inequality of power in this marriage and family setting, mitigated initially by Anna's concern for their infant son (rather than for herself), and by the charges of assault and battery against Bob (no doubt brought at the insistence of the shelter and likely not by Anna). To support her growing power to take control of her life, the life of her son, and of her marriage, Anna has the shelter, Kathy, and the courts, and her own sense of relief that she has found safety, at least temporarily, through the exercise of her own agential power, by making a choice and taking action.

Against Anna's own agency, stand her husband, her parents, her friends, her view of the Bible's teaching about the subordination of wives to husbands, and her internalized beliefs about her church's teaching about marriage. She also wonders if God hates her for using her power on behalf of her son, and, indirectly, on her own behalf. Given her social system and religious beliefs, her act of power, or of "choice," as Kathy rightly labels it, is a truly revolutionary act. It is no wonder that she feels precarious and ambivalent. Any act of power, especially one that destabilizes the predominant power relationships, is always met with counterforce and has mixed consequences. In Anna, we see that shame, or "embarrassment," is the psycho-spiritual force that undercuts her power, and ties her to the existing social pattern that is so harmful for her. Later, we will explore the source of the power to break the hold of shame, but for now it is critical to note that one agential act, as important as it is, is the beginning rather than the end of changing a destructive pattern of relationship. It is also important to note that Bob, while an agent accountable for using power violently against his wife, is also powerless with respect to alcohol and may be under the dominating power of other agents. We do not have enough information to gauge this, but longer-term pastoral care, and fuller social analysis, would have to sort out more incisively the powerful pressures that limit his agency to such violent expressions.

In addition to the power dynamics of those caught in this symptomatic crisis, it is important to recognize that the pastoral agent is also embedded within a network of power arrangements. It is therefore impossible for the pastoral caregiver to be neutral with respect to power in the helping relationship. Kathy is not neutral, even though she rightly concerns herself that she not use her power impositionally. From the beginning, Kathy enters this pastoral situation from the power position of the battered women's shelter, which takes an advocacy role for women. Kathy affirms Anna's decision to take action, and to change herself and her relational patterns by doing so. She affirms God's relation to her action, and challenges those who draw upon the Christian tradition to victimize women through violence. Anna, in spite of ambivalence and ongoing questions about God's attitude toward her action, feels relief and increased self-worth. She says that she likes talking to Kathy because Kathy looks at her, rather than down on her. Kathy, in spite of some minor exceptions, has established a relatively more egalitarian relationship than that of the shelter as a whole, and certainly more than that which is found in the social network out of which Anna comes.

There is yet another dimension of power evident from this verbatim. There are core theological issues and approaches in conflict with one another. It is a struggle over which hermeneutics will guide the care that is to be given. Kathy operates on the hermeneutical principle of justice that says, "one person is not to abuse another." Actions of conscience to protect the vulnerable and to get help for the abuser are justified in God's eyes by the extent to which they bring about a greater measure of relational justice for all in the network. Anna, by contrast, has internalized an ethic of loyalty to tradition and the subordinated obedience of women and children to male authority in marriage, ecclesia, and society. In this respect, an act of pastoral care is an act of hermeneutical power that may engage conflictually with other modes of interpretation and ecclesial power. Pastoral care, therefore, engages power dynamics, and itself constitutes a challenge to certain predominant power arrangements in individuals, the church and the larger social order.

SEPARATIVE POWER AND SYMPTOMATIC CRISES

From Anna's case, we can see that imbalances and struggles between conflicting hermeneutics of power underlie symptomatic behavior driving persons to seek pastoral care. The symptoms arise, not from the reality of power–as though power is somehow negative and unwarranted in human relationships–but from the way power is arranged concretely and existentially. Agential and receptive power have many possible configurations. There are many possible value judgments relevant to these configurations. I would like to suggest that there are two dominant modes of arranging agential and receptive power affecting pastoral care. These are opposed, and need to be adjudicated conceptually and strategically in the practice of care.

The first, and largely negative, mode is what I am calling, "separative power." The term, "separative," is adapted from feminist theologian Catherine Keller's book, *From a Broken Web: Separation, Sexism, and Self* (Boston: Beacon Press, 1986). In this book, Keller argues that the normative model of selfhood in Western religion, psychology and culture is dominated by patriarchal patterns that prize control, heroism, transcendence and repulsion toward chaos and unpredictability. The normative self is the self that has the power to defeat the enemy, conquer new vistas, successfully separate from origins and master the challenges facing the hero on the journey away, and back again. Keller calls this the "separative self."[5] For our purposes, the separative self is based upon and embodies "separative power," or the power to disconnect, control, and render the other subservient to one's own purposes. It is ultimately power over, or power against, others. It is agential in its dominant mode, though it finally becomes a receptor of the resources and ultimately the very selfhood of those it renders powerless. According to Keller, separative selfhood is the source of misogyny and violence against women in western civil and religious culture.

Keller argues that the complement to separative selfhood is "soluble" selfhood. In order for the separative self to come into being and to preserve its life, it must be against that which is different. Keller identifies this other as the female, or feminine, characterized by chaos, unpredictability, creativity within context, and fecundity. For the separative self, the female and the gods and goddesses historically connected with female activity must be overcome. The separative self arises from the exercise of power that renders the female a monster and the male a conquering hero. In Keller's words, ". . . it is by killing the monster that the male establishes her monstrosity and his heroism. But as monster, she is *his* symptom, *his* dread and his monstrosity. Yet she is also symbol of the lost selfhood of which her one time power was an outer sign."[6] Thus, for Keller, the separative self works on the soluble self as a "solvent," which accounts for "women's tendency to dissolve emotionally and devotionally into the other . . ." Indeed, in the case of Anna noted above, we see that she is struggling to differentiate from a structure of selfhood that dissolves her power. For her to make a choice against this structure makes her even more vulnerable to it. It is only as her pastoral helper suggests that perhaps her actions are God's way of getting help for her husband that she is able to tolerate her agency. Yet, the danger of this formulation is that it justifies her agential power only in terms of its benefit toward others, rather than including her own welfare and the character of the whole social fabric in assessing the moral impact of her actions.

Shame is one of the most potent solvents by which separative power operates. Anna feels some relief in acting with power in her system, but this is quickly countered by a sense of shame for her situation. She wonders if her actions against her husband's abusive power were morally justified. This leads quickly and directly to the issue of guilt and forgiveness in this pastoral situation. The core idea of Christian forgiveness is "to release" from debt, bondage, and the power of the past, to the freedom of new life with God and neighbor. But, under the dynamics of separative power, activated and maintained by shame, the good news of forgiveness becomes a moral burden placed upon the powerless by their abusers, and sometimes by their caregivers. In this case, Anna is more worried about her lack of obedience to her husband than his failure to keep the injunction to be Christ-like to his wife and children. She is more concerned with her accountability for leaving him and having him arrested, than for his act of violence against her person. Her shame, and the implied imperative that she forgive, keeps her morally accountable in a manner exceeding the accountability that he has for his actions. She is further dissolved, while he may be absolved without repentance and restitution.

A fuller examination of the dynamics of power in the process of forgiveness helps us see more clearly how separative power might employ the central affirmations of the Christian tradition to hurt rather than heal. John Patton, a pastoral theologian and past president of the American Association of Pastoral Counselors, has written a very insightful book on forgiveness from a pastoral-theological vantage point. In *Is Human Forgiveness Possible?: A Pastoral Care Perspective* (Abingdon Press, 1985), Patton says that forgiveness has been wrongly linked with guilt. He says that the core issue underlying forgiveness is shame. The difference is this. Guilt is connected to specific acts and attitudes, and is more readily handled by rational means, as well as by catharsis and confession.[7] On the other hand, shame involves "the vulnerability of the whole self," that comes into being by an act by another who violates the self, leaving it feeling inadequate and incomplete. This deeper wounding of the self–in Keller's terms, this rendering the self, soluble by the agential power of the separative hero, can only be repaired over time by the slow growth of an empathic relationship. Since the self is now lacking something, it does not have the power by which it is able to offer forgiveness. It is in bondage to the injuring party.

To protect against this debt, or bondage, the wounded self has many defenses that must be overcome for the possibility of forgiveness to emerge. These, like the story with which I opened this article, function to hide the true situation and to create the illusion of power and self-preservation. Patton identifies three defenses against shame that make the relational discovery of forgiveness impossible, and, in terms of power, keep persons in a separative, isolated and estranged mode. These defenses are rage, power, and righteousness. Rage, arising from a severe narcissistic injury, empowers the sense of self, and compensates for the injury at the core of one's being. It masks the injury and gives the illusion of power over the other. Righteousness helps persons avoid their own shame by "searching for the other's guilt."[8] It is another form of gaining power over the injuring party, through perfectionism, innocence and blaming. Power, as a defense against shame and forgiveness, takes two forms. It may take the form of withholding forgiveness as a moral weapon, a trump card, over the injuring party. Or, it may take the form of powerlessness, thereby controlling the other and the situation by inaction or the seeming inability to act. Those who do family pastoral care well know the ways that individuals in a family, and the family itself, maintain chronic symptoms as a way of gaining power over the other family members, as well as over the caregiver.

The question of forgiveness can thereby become allied with power in such a manner that both separation or solubility, or some combination of each, prevails, and the creative vitality of both the offended and offending party is diminished rather than enhanced. Without attention to these power dynamics, the caregiver may become ineffectual, or, worse, use the central tenets of their theological tradition to contribute to the legitimation of power used as defense against shame rather than as a basis for healing the offended, holding the offender accountable, and finding release from bondage to abuse and its aftermath. If in the mind of the caregiver forgiveness is linked only with catharsis on the part of the victim and not also with the restitution and other steps required by the perpetrator to resolve the injury they have caused, then victims who substitute rage, power and righteousness are likely to be re-victimized by a community that would like to see them "get over it and move on." Their attitudes, rather than the offending injury, may become the identified problem. But, if forgiveness is ultimately based upon the restoration of a destroyed or impaired self, then the caregiver will be patient and not impose a psycho-spiritual and morally impossible task upon the injured. There will be an appropriate recognition that the shamed party needs defenses, and that perpetrators need accountability. Power is in the service of both. Attitudes such as power, rage and righteousness, therefore, may serve both necessary defensive needs, as well as provide an essential moral basis for protesting abuse and holding abusers accountable.

CONNECTIVE POWER AND HUMAN VITALITY

If separative and soluble power configurations are problematic, what might be offered instead? What form of power, and of power arrangements, are normative then for pastoral caregivers? I suggest, again following Catherine Keller, that "connective power" is an alternative to either separative or soluble power in human selfhood and relationships. For Keller, the connective self is an alternative for men and women that allows for relationship without subordination and domination on the one hand, or separativeness and solubility, on the other. Founded upon a theological orientation that posits the irreducible interconnectedness, or braiding, of life in the mutual co-creation of one another, Keller argues that the connective self weaves together into new harmonies those elements that have been separated and/or opposed. She reconfigures the personal and the public, the body and soul, the one and the many, and the now and the not-yet into a new dialectical unity that allows for distinctiveness without oppositional separation.[9] For Keller the image of a spider continually spinning and re-spinning a web, weaving a delicate fabric to support and preserve life best illustrates her view of connectivity.[10] The brokenness of the web, as disclosed in symptomatic behavior, "continues to unveil the connections between the power structures of patriarchy and the psychopolitics of separative selfhood. . . . " But, the web also reveals that 'the relations between things are as delicate as spider's silk, known only instinctively, with profound indirection–yet "strong enough to hang a bridge on."[11]

Building upon Keller, we may regard the metaphor of the web as a hermeneutical device by which to assess the nature of the power dynamics arising in the context of pastoral care. Estrangement, depression, ambivalence, domestic and sexual violence, the struggle to discover forgiveness, and the myriad of other symptoms leading persons to need and seek care, result from the imbalances in power, operating separatively. They reflect unjust relationality in which the good of some is at the expense or to the detriment of others. For anything like healing, reconciliation, forgiveness, and growth to take place, there must be an underlying connective power. This connective power begins in the genuine empathic joining of the helper to each of the parties seeking care. It values rather than condemns or instrumentalizes the unique selfhood of the other. It extends to a perceptive assessment of the nature and sources of the brokenness in the relational web, and the capacity to withstand the assaults on the helping relationship by those operating out of a separative mindset. Finally, connective power moves to a creative re-spinning, or reweaving, of the broken web into a restored whole, or creating novel and surprising patterns altogether.

Returning momentarily to Patton's discussion of forgiveness, it is clear that to move from injury and defense–to discover forgiveness–one must have a corrective experience at the core of the self where the injury took place and shame rendered the self impotent. This correction is made possible by an empathic embrace by the caregiver, and the recognition that the injured party is at some fundamental level no different than the injuring party. Human connection empowers human healing, and the capacity for forgiveness is discovered as a gift of healing in relationship rather than a singular moral act by a separative self who by simple will and rationality can give or withhold forgiveness.

What are the theological grounds for affirming the viability of connective power in the practice of care? I have already mentioned Catherine Keller's metaphysics of a relational and ongoing creation as the foundation for the connective self and its spinning new worlds. In her process theological metaphysics, God is the great spinner who participates with every other creature in weaving and re-weaving the web of life. Paul Tillich has helped us to see that divine love is the foundation for uniting the separated and overcoming estrangement with acceptance.[12] Feminist and other liberation theologians have developed the concept of "relational justice" to guide our caregiving efforts in the face of oppressive power arrangements.[13] The concept of relational justice provides a natural link between the critique of power in the Jewish and Christian prophetic tradition, and the specific acts of Christian pastoral care. Finally, Jurgen Moltmann helps us to regain a sense of the relationship between God's Spirit and the Christian Trinity to the dynamics of connective power. For Moltmann, "the energies of the Spirit" are experienced charismatically, and operate as "vitalizing energies, because they bring us to life."[14] He links this coming to life with love, and links divine energy to the connective power of eros. By eros he means, "the force which holds the world together and keeps it alive, anthropologically and cosmologically: the power of attraction which unites, and the individual weight which simultaneously distinguishes." For Moltmann, the effect of the spirit is to bring joy and peace to the hearts of people. Such peace leads to resistance toward the abuse of separative power, and promotes connective power throughout the social and natural order. He says, "For the person who experiences the peace of God 'in the heart' begins to hope for peace on earth, and therefore begins to resist peacelessness, armaments and war in the world of human beings, and exploitation and devastation in the world of nature."[15] Further, Moltmann affirms that the healing of the sick and of broken relationships rooted in "the healing power of the divine Spirit," and "in the context of faith . . . are signs of the new creation and the rebirth of life."[16] All healing is grounded in God, and in the ongoing participation of God in the life of the world.

Based upon these profound theological themes, the caregiver can rest confidently in the reality of a power not entirely our own, but persistently available to overcome injurious configurations of separative power. The power we affirm does not result in pseudo-connectivity and tentative distance, as in the case of the Pope and the leader of the Roman Jewish community. Nor does it have to take sides with one or another form of separative power contending for domination, as in the case reported above by Kathy. Rather, it can seek to find the terms on which each self might be in right relationship with every other self, in a new connective whole. Anna can be helped to find ways to hold her husband Bob accountable for his drinking and his battering, without subverting her own vitality on the one hand, or putting Bob into a subordinated position relative to her righteousness and potential of using forgiveness as a weapon, on the other hand. Connective empathy might empower the spinning of a new web for this family, or to help them leave it without undue estrangement and risk. I do not know how this situation finally turned out, but I have seen similar situations resolved as power is rearranged, shame overcome through genuine healing connections, and forgiveness and reconciliation emerge through care, accountability, and learning non-violent ways to control conflict, aggression, and impulses.

CONCLUSION

Power is inevitably pervasive in human life. Its arrangements have vital significance for human welfare. When arranged in such a manner that reinforces symptoms of violence and domination, power functions unjustly to separate and dissolve healthy and positive relational patterns. The pastoral caregiver serves others best when he or she uses the power of the helping relationship to arrange power dynamics so that they contribute to human liberation from violence and oppression, and eventuate in creative alternatives to domination and subordination.

NOTES

1. This article is adapted from a lecture given at the Escola Superior de Theologia Sao Leopoldo, Brazil in August, 1997 "A dinâmica do poder ma assistência pastoral," in Fundamentos Teólogicos do Aconselhamento, Editora Sinodal, San Leopoldo, Brazil, 1998, pp. 7-20. It is used here with permission.

2. See James N. Poling, *The Abuse of Power: A Theological Problem* (Nashville: Abingdon Press, 1991, Pamela D. Couture and Rodney J. Hunter, Eds., *Pastoral Care and Social Conflict* (Nashville: Abingdon Press, 1995), and Kathleen J. Greider, *Reckoning with Aggression* (Louisville: Westminster John Knox Press, 1997).

3. Bonnie J. Miller-McLemore, "The Human Web: Reflections on the State of Pastoral Theology," *Christian Century* (April 7): 366-69.

4. A modified version of the case can be found in Larry Kent Graham, *Care of Persons, Care of Worlds: A Psychosystems Approach to Pastoral Care and Counseling* (Nashville: Abingdon Press, 1992), pp. 29-32.

5. Catherine Keller, *From a Broken Web: Separation, Sexism, and Self* (Boston: Beacon Press, 1986), p. 7-46.

6. Ibid., p. 62.

7. John Patton, *Is Human Forgiveness Possible?: A Pastoral Care Perspective* (Nashville: Abingdon Press, 1985), p. 39.

8. Ibid, p. 93.

9. Keller, p. 225.

10. Ibid., p. 217.

11. Ibid., p. 218.

12. Paul Tillich. Love Power and Justice: Ontological Analyses and Ethical Applications (NY: Oxford University Press, 1954).

13. See Carter Heyward, *Touching Our Strength The Erotic as Power and the Love of God* (San Francisco: HarperColling, 1989), J. Michael Clark, *Beyond our Ghetto: Gay Liberation in Ecological Perspective* (Cleveland: The Pilgrim Press, 1993), and Larry Kent Graham, *Discovering Images of God: Narratives of Care with Lesbians and Gays* (Louisville: Westminster John Knox Press, 1997).

14. Jurgen Moltmann, The Spirit of Life: A Universal Affirmation, Minneapolis, 1992), p. 196.

15. Ibid., p. 154.

16. Ibid., p. 159.

You Know What the Bible Says: A Proposal for Engaging Scripture with Male Abusers

Richard Wallace

SUMMARY. In this article the author explores the uses and misuses of the Bible in confronting African American men about violence. Following narrative and hermeneutical methods, he exposes tendencies to violence in the Bible, and suggests alternative approaches to reading the Bible within the African American churches. *[Article copies available for a fee from The Haworth Document Delivery Service: 1-800-HAWORTH. E-mail address: <docdelivery@haworthpress.com> Website: <http://www.HaworthPress.com> © 2002 by The Haworth Press, Inc. All rights reserved.]*

KEYWORDS. Sexual and domestic violence, African American male identity, African American theology

Two guys were arguing about their knowledge of the Lord's prayer. The first guy said to the second, "I bet five bucks you don't know the Lord's Prayer." The second guy says, "You're on," and started reciting:

Now I lay me down to sleep
I pray the Lord my soul to keep

[Haworth co-indexing entry note]: "You Know What the Bible Says: A Proposal for Engaging Scripture with Male Abusers." Wallace, Richard. Co-published simultaneously in *Journal of Religion & Abuse* (The Haworth Pastoral Press, an imprint of The Haworth Press, Inc.) Vol. 4, No. 3, 2002, pp. 89-106; and: *Men's Work in Preventing Violence Against Women* (ed: James Newton Poling, and Christie Cozad Neuger) The Haworth Pastoral Press, an imprint of The Haworth Press, Inc., 2002, pp. 89-106. Single or multiple copies of this article are available for a fee from The Haworth Document Delivery Service [1-800-HAWORTH, 9:00 a.m. - 5:00 p.m. (EST). E-mail address: docdelivery@haworthpress.com].

http://www.haworthpress.com/store/product.asp?sku=J154
© 2002 by The Haworth Press, Inc. All rights reserved.
10.1300/J154v4n03_08

If I die before I wake
I pray the Lord my soul to take.

The first guy says, "I'll be damned. You do know the Lord's prayer," as he hands over five dollars. I am reminded of this story when I hear the unexamined and uncontested attributes that function as biblical truths. For instance, how many times have we heard someone say, "You know what the Bible says–God takes care of those who take of themselves," which then becomes authoritative.

I'm particularly conscious of this in the area of domestic violence where, according to Melody Moody who works with male abusers:

> ...even men who say they have no spiritual belief system will still use the Christian scripture to justify their abusive behavior when it is convenient for them. "They'll tell me 'According to the Bible, I'm the head of my wife, the boss. So I can't let her do the things she's doing, because she'll start thinking she's the boss.[1]

While the Bible may be regarded as characteristically patriarchal, what is interesting is the appeal to certain texts by those who don't really know the text.

This was demonstrated for me in another way when during a seminary class discussion about marital rape one of the students reminded us that according to the Bible the man has certain rights. I found myself wondering, what biblical text gives a man the right to expect and demand sex from his wife any time. Furthermore, I wondered if this student who was an African American would make the similar argument about slavery.

In all of this, I find what Allene Stuart Phy says to be particularly provocative.

> Americans remain, according to the latest Gallup polls, among the most religious people in the world. The majority of U.S. citizens, and Canadians too, also claim to be devoted to the Bible, even though many actually know very little of the scriptures and would indeed be shocked to discover some of the assertions contained therein . . . The culture echoes the Bible at every level, yet actual knowledge of the scriptures is slight and declining even in the Bible-thumping American South. The Bible itself is studied less than ever before, and it may be that it reaches Americans today, for better or worse, largely as it is filtered through popular culture.[2]

The Bible that is filtered through the popular culture is the Bible that Peter Gomes describes as "an American cultural icon, with enormous influence both symbolic and substantial."[3]

I would agree with Phy except in the interim between 1985 to the present there appears to be a resurgence in Bible study. However, I regard the resurgence as somewhat hollow when the only biblical texts that are reflected upon are from the Sunday morning pericopes, which can be described as traveling to a destination where one drives on the interstate all the way–persons may get to where they're going but they miss a lot along the way. Conversely, this resurgence of biblical study can result in getting so bogged down in the minutiae of the biblical text, that it is like one getting lost in the back roads and therefore never getting to one's destination.

In spite of the resurgence in Bible study, the majority of Americans' biblical knowledge is still filtered through the popular culture. This suggests to me that the initial problem is not one of hermeneutics alone, but also literacy in the sense of not knowing the diversity of the Biblical text. Therefore, the problem is how to develop knowledge of scripture that goes beyond what is filtered through the popular culture.

As it relates to male abusers, what is filtered through the popular culture suggests the image of a sieve, where the size and shape of the holes determines what gets caught and what passes through. Through my work with the "Men's Messages Action Team" in the Twin Cities of Minnesota, I am concerned about what gets filtered out. More specifically, why do men who don't even claim to be Christian know certain biblical texts that will never challenge their abusive behaviors?

I recall very vividly the reaction of an African American male after a worship service where one of the "texts of terror," as identified by Phyllis Trible,[4] was read. He was upset because it was read while children were present. I remember being initially quite amused with his reaction because it made me think of how one might construct a rating system so that only PG texts would be read. However, as I did some further reflection, I thought that maybe his concern could lead to a changed understanding of the Bible. In one sense, his reaction was not unlike the reaction of first year seminarians whose understanding of the Bible gets deconstructed. What was actually being deconstructed, for this individual and the first year seminarians, was the Bible that is filtered through the popular culture.

The Bible that is filtered through the popular culture excluded these texts of terror. However, there are similar exclusions in the public worship of churches that mirror the popular culture. Lester Meyer, in an article entitled "A Lack of Laments in the Church's use of the Psalter," addresses this when he writes:

> Upon examination of the common lectionary of the mainline Christian churches it is discovered that the lament type of psalm is scarcely represented. This fact compromises the church's liturgical capacity to address the problems of God's absence and the Christian's suffering. For this reason these psalms should be restored to the lectionary for regular worship.[5]

The exclusion of these lament psalms from the church's liturgical practice has meant that the people were denied access to a resource that challenged the popular culture. Perhaps this is evident through the many times that pastoral care providers have heard someone express their anger to God and almost immediately dismissed what they were feeling because it was too unacceptable. In other words, this is what I'm feeling but I shouldn't be feeling this way. One doesn't have to overly tax one's memory to recall some of the ways that the popular culture promotes and reinforces the notion of God as unapproachable and distant.

The Bible that comes to us filtered through the popular culture is an homogenized text that tolerates little or no ambiguity. Walter Brueggemann's assessment of the lack of the laments speaks directly to this point.

> Much Christian piety and spirituality is romantic and unreal in its positiveness. As children of the Enlightenment, we have censored and selected around the voice of darkness and disorientation, seeking to go from strength to strength, from victory to victory . . . It is no wonder that the church had intuitively avoided these psalms. They lead us into the presence of God where everything is not polite and civil. They cause us to think unthinkable thoughts and utter unutterable words. Perhaps worst, they lead us away from the comfortable religious claims of "modernity" in which everything is managed and controlled. In our modern experiences, but probably also in every successful and affluent culture, it is believed that enough power and knowledge can tame the terror and eliminate the darkness.[6]

When we consider the significant numbers of male abusers who have themselves been the victims of abuse, then it may be seen how the exclusion of the lament psalms may directly relate. Brueggemann says that the lament psalms can provide a formfulness for grief.

> All the uses of this form in Israel or elsewhere insist that grief is formful. It can be supervised according to community forms which make it bearable and manageable in the community. The griever is kept in community or returned to the community by having it articulated that this experience does not lie outside the legitimate scope of the community. It is not an abyss either anomic [meaning social instability caused by an erosion of standards or values] or chaotic. By the use of the form the grief experience is made bearable and, and it hoped, meaningful. The form makes the experience formful just when it appears to be formless and therefore deathly and destructive.[7]

Although the case could be made that abuse is related to grief, it is not my intent to reduce abuse to grief. However, imagine a male victim of abuse finding words in the lament psalms that give voice to the unspeakable. Can the readers imagine the possible empowerment for a victim of abuse from the words of Psalm 13:1-2:

> How long, O Lord? Will you forget forever?
> How long will you hide your face from me?
> How long must I bear pain in my soul, and have sorrow in my heart all day long?
> How long shall my enemy be exalted over me? (NRSV)

What I am suggesting, is that the inclusion of the lament psalms in the church's public worship may greatly assist those who are victims of abuse by providing a formfulness for their pain–that they need not suffer in secret disconnected from the community. Furthermore, imagine the powerful connection that can be made when one realizes that through their own abusive behavior they have become like "the enemy that was exalted over them."

When the Bible that is filtered through the popular culture, which may be particularly evident in the church's liturgical practice that excludes the lament psalms, the church not only accommodates to the abuser but contributes to the ongoing normalization of abuse. The Bible that is filtered through the popular culture maintains the status quo, and in particular the gender power arrangements. This is what Gomes also describes as "the Bible's use as a textbook for the status quo."[8]

The Bible that is filtered through the popular culture has often been used to victimize others, in particular women, people of color, and gays and lesbians. More specifically, particular Biblical texts have been used to justify the subordinate status of women, the inferiority of Africans and Native Americans in order to justify slavery and the conquest and subjugation of native peoples, and the exclusion and subsequent oppression and suppression of same sex oriented persons. The consequence of the filterization is that these texts are regarded as definitive Biblical text. In effect, it is an attempt to apply the homogenization and essentializing processes of the popular culture to the Bible.

In order to counter these processes that resulted in their victimization, women, people of color, and gays and lesbians have developed approaches to the Bible that appealed to its heterogeneous reality-in effect, saying "but, that's not all that the Bible says."

A noted illustration of this approach at the time of slavery is recorded by Gayraud Wilmore:

> CC. Jones reported in the Tenth Report of the Association for the Religious Instruction of the Negroes in Liberty County, Georgia, an interesting incident in this regard.

> I was preaching to a large congregation on the Epistles to Philemon; and when I insisted on fidelity and obedience as Christian virtues in servants, and upon the authority of Paul, condemned the practice of running away, one-half of my audience deliberately rose up and walked off with themselves; and those who remained looked anything but satisfied with the preacher or his doctrine. After dismissal, there was no small stir among them; some solemnly declared that there was no such Epistle in the Bible; others, that it was not the Gospel.[9]

At this level, the slaves rejected the homogenization and essentializing of scripture in these particular texts, regarding with suspicion anything from the Bible that sought to make the current social arrangements of the enslavement of Africans necessary, as an ordination of God.

Unfortunately, this complex hermeneutical method of understanding the Bible often does not include challenging the social arrangements where women are subjugated to men. That is to say while most African American men can recognize the slave's hermeneutic of suspicion with regard to the text that made their enslavement and subjugation a divine necessity, they are unable to apply it to other attempts to justify social arrangements in the name of God. Jacqueline Grant, the noted womanist theologian,[10] early on addresses this immaturity when she writes:

> . . . Black men have accepted without question the patriarchal structures of the White society as normative for the Black community. How can a Black minister preach in a way which advocates St. Paul's dictum concerning women while ignoring or repudiating his dictum concerning slaves?[11]

Kristen E. Kvam, Linda S. Schearing, and Valerie H. Ziegler have written an amazing book in which they delineate the various ways that Genesis 1-3 has been interpreted and filtered through the popular culture, and reinterpret it to challenge this filteration. What makes their book so significant are the three lenses from which they write–Christian, Jewish, and Muslim. The title of this book is *Eve & Adam: Jewish, Christian, and Muslim Readings on Genesis and Gender.* Their opening words in the introduction seem to be quite germane to the discussion.

> In this book, we examine Genesis 1-3 and the ways that interpreters have used this text to define and enforce gender roles. We watch for instances in which interpreters have used Genesis 1-3 to confirm cultural presuppositions about gender roles and identity. We also note cases in which readers have found in Genesis understandings that moved them to challenge social norms.[12]

In effect, their examination provides some historical insights into how Genesis 1-3 has been filtered through the popular culture's presuppositions about gender roles. The fact that they also examine the understandings of Genesis that have provided a challenge to the status quo is particularly germane to the discussion because it may provide some insights into how to counter the effects of the filters behavior that abusive males use to justify their behavior. What is being challenged is the line of reasoning–the Bible says that men are in charge so you're supposed to do whatever I tell you to do." This may sound like an intentional oversimplification of what men believe, but it is precisely what I often hear in groups for male abusers.

While Kvam et al. provide an extensive and thorough inventory of the various ways that Genesis 1-3 has been filtered through the cultural presuppositions about gender and identity in Judaism, Christianity, and

Islam, the chapter towards the end of their book "Twentieth-Century Readings: The Debates Continue," speaks most directly to the overall discussion. They write in the introduction–In no previous century has concern for establishing men as the 'head' of women been more pronounced." This is not surprising, given the fact that the twentieth century was a time when the transition of gender roles and identity was great.

This assertion by Kvam et al. relates tangentially to a controversial theory, which argues somewhat differently. Frank Pittman, III represents this perspective when he writes:

> However, the most consistent factor in the nature of men who are violent toward their wives is that they have an overdeveloped sense of gender. They believe they should be powerful, successful, adored, served, and desired-and they know they are not. They experience themselves as powerless, and they may be ashamed of that and want to deny it, or they may want to be reassured that it doesn't matter. Feeling like failures, they want to be seen as important so they can be loved.[13]

In other words, the male whose social position was such that he could not exercise any power or authority over others and was always the victim of other's authority was still the head of his own home. However, given the transitions occurring in the society with regard to gender roles and identity, the bastion of individual male dominance within the family is being threatened.

For Kvam et al., the debate is framed by the contrast between hierarchal and egalitarian interpretations. When the Bible is filtered through popular cultures that are hierarchical, they maintain the status quo and its particular power arrangement–namely patriarchal hierarchy. Conversely Kvam et al. argue that the Bible is now being filtered through the popular culture where gender equality is being promoted.

Kvam et al, demonstrates the contrast by including the perspective of those who still believe in gender hierarchy and hope to preserve it in a more acceptable and less violent form. This perspective would argue that gender hierarchy is biblical and must be preserved because of the authority of the Bible. Kvam et al illustrate this perspective in their discussion of the "Danvers Statement," which was drafted in Danvers,

Massachusetts in 1987 at a meeting of The Council on Biblical Manhood and Womanhood. The following citation is from the rationale that includes ten points of which points one, three, eight, nine, and ten are cited.[14]

> We have been moved in our purpose by the following contemporary developments which we observe with deep concern:
>
> 1. The widespread uncertainty and confusion in our culture regarding the complimentary differences between masculinity and femininity;
>
> 3. the increasing promotion given to feminist egalitarianism with accompanying distortions or neglect of the glad harmony portrayed in Scripture between the loving, humble leadership of redeemed husbands and the intelligent, willing support of that leadership by redeemed wives;
>
> 8. the increasing prevalence and acceptance of hermeneutical oddities devised to reinterpret apparently plain meanings of Biblical texts;
>
> 9. the consequent threat to Biblical authority as the clarity of Scripture is jeopardized and the accessibility of its meaning to ordinary people is withdrawn into the restrictive realm of technical ingenuity.
>
> 10. and behind all this the apparent accommodation of some within the church to the spirit of the age at the expense of winsome, radical Biblical authenticity which in the power of the Holy Spirit may reform rather than reflect our ailing culture.

Here Kvam et al. argue that accommodation to contemporary culture in its emphasis of gender equality undermines the Abrahamic faith traditions and contributes to violent relationships between women and men.

In contrast I appeal to H. Richard Niebuhr's category of Christ and Culture in Paradox.[15] According to this view, there is no culture, with its attendant cultural practices and social arrangements, that is inherently good. Every culture must be challenged by the revelation of truth in the Bible. Every interpretation of the Bible must be challenged by the contemporary issues of contemporary believers.

The Danver's statement and other similar perspectives seem to be indicative of the category of Christ above culture.[16] Although, there does seem to be some movement, albeit slight, towards Christ and culture in paradox in the explicit condemnation of male abusive behavior by evangelicals, which was so conspicuously absent in the past, it is based on the assumption that there is still something redeemable about patriarchy–the problem is not that men are in charge but the way that they exercise their charge. Susan T. Foh, author of Woman and the Word of God: A Response to Biblical Feminism writes:

> This understanding of Genesis 3:16 is corroborated by experience. If it is translated "and he shall rule over you" (RSV), the words are not true; not every husband rules his wife. Instead, marriages are filled with strife and discontent. The loss of the wife's willing submission and the husband's loving "rule" each have two opposite aberrations. Wives manipulate and sometimes dominate their husbands; and some wives, losing all sense of their own worth, live only through their husbands and children. Some husbands, abdicating their position, absent themselves from the home through work, sports or alcohol; and some husbands physically or emotionally abuse their wives.

> With this understanding of Genesis 3:16 in view, Paul, in Ephesians 5:22-33, focuses on the areas where wives and husbands tend to sin. As a result of sin, wives no longer naturally submit themselves to their husbands, so Paul says, "Wives, submit yourselves to your husbands, as to the Lord" (Eph 5:22 NIV). In their struggle to rule, husbands tend to resort to any means at their disposal, so Paul forestalls these "blows" with "Husbands, love your wives, as Christ loved the church and gave himself up for her." (Eph 5:25 RSV)[17]

Just as the argument for a more humane slavery cannot be supported by appeal to the Bible, so patriarchy cannot be preserved by suggesting that the Bible calls for a more humane inequality between men and women.

In contrast, I argue for a process of "depatriarchalizing."[18] Ultimately, God's will is not dependent upon patriarchy or for that matter any human social arrangement. This is what some liberation theologians call "the non-necessity of the present order." For men, and abusive men in particular, it is important to imagine a way of being a male without having to be in control.

Coupled with the non-necessity of patriarchy is the non-necessity of the patriarchal metaphors. This has been the contribution of Renita Weems in her book *Battered Love: Marriage, Sex, and Violence in the Hebrew Prophets*. When Weems writes about the metaphor of Israel as the unfaithful wife and God as the betrayed husband, one is mindful of the stories that can be read in newspapers daily or viewed nightly on television news.

> On the matter of the unique bond that exists between God and Is-rael, the marriage metaphor (like the parent-child metaphor) con-veyed the notion that the covenant relationship between God and Israel created a quasi-familial bond between the two where love and trust undergirded the relationship. But at times the love was a menacing sort, one that drove a husband (God) to plead, cajole, stalk, and threaten his wife (Israel). In this image, divine love was as uncompromising and jealous as it was compassionate and ten-der. The husband's love was fueled by some very definite notions about the rights and privileges of the husband. Having as he did the power to divorce his wife, the authority to haul her before the cult on charges of infidelity, and the right to his wife's exclusive sexu-ality, the husband clearly had the upper hand in the relationship. In fact, the metaphor is comprehensible only if one concedes that in-deed the husband was fully within his rights to retaliate physically against his wife for her offenses against him.[19]

This point is echoed in news stories about a man who kills his wife, chil-dren, and then himself because she was leaving him. It is not that there is a causal relationship between these metaphors and men who abuse, but that they are part of a whole language of culture–the ideological super-structure. Weems says that "metaphors originate in social contexts and reinforce social contexts."[20]

Jeffrey Hossick, a pastoral counselor, takes this a step further through his work with metaphors in his doctoral dissertation "An Understanding of a Contribution of Metaphor and Music in the Healing of the Isolation Dynamic."

In the introduction, Hossick writes:

> Further reflection on Scripture records times when the prophets were instructed to use metaphors to express God's dis-content with Israel. Amos uses metaphor to communicate God's contention against the nations of Israel. Jesus uses metaphor in the parables, and the I Am statements from John's gospel. This points to Jesus communicating truth in metaphoric models.

> Reflecting upon the scriptural use of music and metaphor, stories such as David's lust for Bathsheba (2 Samuel 11), the rape

of Tamar (2 Samuel 13), the Man at the pool who was asked if he wanted to be well (John 5), have been used in a sex offender treatment program as metaphors of self. The narratives were used as case studies with the purpose of providing insight into how behaviors develop in sexual crimes.[21]

Hossick's point suggests an approach for work for abusive males–particularly, the story of David's lust for Bathsheba.

Hossick's approach relies upon the methodology of Gregory Bateson "who shows that a multiplicity of metaphors often adds depth to understanding life."[22] Specifically, he is utilizing Bateson's methodology of abduction that borrows metaphors from one system for use in another. Hossick is using Bateson's abduction method "to link the three fields of his study, music, metaphor and the psycho-social-spiritual dynamics of healing shame, highlighting the common elements and possible uses of these elements for addressing spiritual, psychological and emotional problems. The most important aspect of Bateson's methodology for the sake of this discussion may be how it allows for the fluidity of metaphors. This fluidity is evident when Hossick looks at "the process of how metaphors interact with each other creating the emergence of new metaphors."[23]

Hossick's assertion that "healing comes through the changing of perspective, the opening of the model to new possibilities,"[24] can be applied to the abusive male. In this particular instance, the task is to change the behavior through the introduction of contrasting metaphors. Hossick's following assertion is descriptive of this task.

> Metaphors are the icons of understanding. They help to construct new meaning, while at the same time eventually needing themselves to be deconstructed. Metaphors have a life span of usefulness. They are born, serve their purpose, and then make way for other metaphors. It is when the meaning of the metaphor is not released to make way for new metaphors that the dynamic system of metaphor, hermeneutics and identity becomes closed.[25]

Speaking from a personal experience, Hossisk is describing my experience when I read Renita Weems' book *Battered Love: Marriage, Sex, and Violence in the Hebrew Prophets*. The metaphor of Israel as the unfaithful wife and God as the betrayed husband was embedded in my preaching. Weems opened to me, albeit not without some pain, a new model with new possibilities. The pain was the result of the process of growth that Hossick describes negatively: "when the meaning of the metaphor is not released to make way for new metaphors."

In a sense, the male who uses the Bible filtered through the popular culture to justify his abusive behavior is challenged not only at the level of cultural metaphors but also at the level of the personal. This never occurs without a certain amount of pain.

Hossick relies upon the work of Paul Ricoeur, [26] a noted philosopher, who coined the familiar phrase, hermeneutics of suspicion:

> Ricoeur offers a challenge through the question. Are we willing to be open to receive new metaphors, even if the old ones are still working? Are we willing to shift from a definitive methodology to an interactive one? Are we willing to be disoriented so that we may re-orient ourselves? . . . One of the challenges Ricoeur presents is to deconstruct old views with the purpose of reconstructing new ones. It is the process of moving the unconscious involuntary will toward conscious voluntary will. It is in seeking new dialogue partners that allows the . . . self-beliefs to be challenged . . . Ricoeur points to the work of the Spirit as the key dialogue partner, Who tries to intervene to create the deconstruction and reconstruction.[27]

When I teach the class on Domestic Violence where I am intentionally challenging old metaphors, I invite the students to identify points of resistance to the new metaphors that they are receiving. I attempt to assist them in identifying the resistance within themselves in order to help them be sensitive to the resistance they will encounter in others when they too introduce new metaphors. This is precisely what happened in the earlier example of the African American male who was visibly upset and agitated as a result of his introduction to one of the texts of terror. He was resisting the deconstruction of his personal metaphors and the cultural metaphors of the Bible filtered through the popular culture, as a result of being confronted with the heterogeneous nature of the Biblical text. This type of disruption and resistance can occur through exposure to the story of David's lust after Bathsheba.

DAVID'S LUST FOR BATHSHEBA

David's lust for Bathsheba in 2 Samuel 11 is itself a metaphor about male sexuality. In the African American community, one sometimes hears a brother justifying his sexual behavior with an underage female by saying, "she was healthy looking." Typically, the offense in traditional interpretations of this passage is more about what David did to Uriah in order to get to Bathsheba. He didn't do Bathsheba wrong but he did Uriah wrong. In effect, he violated another man and stole his property. In fact, in The New Oxford Annotated Bible, published in 1973, the heading for this text is "David's Sin against Uriah." The New Revised Standard Version is a significant improvement "David Commits Adultery with Bathsheba," but it puts the emphasis on breaking marriage vows rather than on violence toward women. So God sends Nathan to David with a parable, a metaphor that challenges David's personal metaphor and perhaps the metaphor of the ideological superstructure. While the metaphor upholds the elements of property which is typical of patriarchal cultures, it also introduces the metaphor of the abuse of power. While I'm not entirely comfortable with this, it could be said that David had abused the power that God has given to him in the first place. Reading this story from Bathsheba's perspective and reflecting upon Nathan's role, hopefully creates the kind of disruption and resistance that leads to transformation for men who want to use Scripture to justify their abusive behavior.

To consider this story from Bathsheba's perspective creates disruption and resistance through the questions that inevitably rise. First and foremost, was she a willing participant in the sexual acts? What power did she have? The Interpreter's Bible Commentary describes it as "Bathsheba's obedience to the King's lust."[28] What happens if Bathsheba rejects David's advances? Can men create an environment where women don't feel comfortable about saying no because of the fear of name-calling or worse?

Reflecting on Nathan's role raises the question of how men can speak to other men, similar to how Nathan spoke to David, about their abuse of power. Nathan used a metaphor in the form of the parable to help David gain some insight into his own behavior. In this regard, I'm interested in how contemporary literature and cinema as metaphor might function similar to Nathan's parable in helping abusive men gain some insight into their own behavior, As such, then, they will have the same potential to similarly convict, as did Nathan's metaphor in the form of the parable–thou art the men.

There are several proposals for how to engage males who use the Bible to justify their abusive behavior with these texts. Initial engagement occurs through the inclusion of these and similar texts that challenge attempts to homogenize the Bible, into the popular culture. Initial engagement is one of the goals Peter Gomes does in his book *The Good Book*, about which he writes in the afterward:

> My third ambition was to encourage those to think again, who think that they know all they need to know about the Bible and what it says and means. This is an invitation not to guilt, although there is much about which to feel guilty, but rather to modesty, one of the more neglected of Christian virtues. One must not use the scriptures as the drunk uses the lamppost–for support rather than for illumination; rather, one reads those inspired words with the very fallible apparatus of fallen human beings. The discussions of anti-Semitism, slavery, women, and homosexuality are not meant to condemn scripture as culturally wrong, or to impugn the faithful ambitions of sincere Christians who may hold differing opinions on these critical matters. These discussions are intended to remind the faithful of the wickedness done in the name of good, of God, and of the Bible, and to make us more cautious and self-conscious of the besetting sin, alas, endemic to the faithful, of confusing our cultural prejudices with immutable will of God, and of using the Bible as a footnote to our convictions. Orthodoxy must never be permitted to become the protective coloration for the self-interest of the status quo; the entire record of scripture cries out against this utterly sinful abuse.[30]

Referring once again to the sieve image, the initial engagement is akin to enlarging the holes through which the Bible is filtered through the popular culture.

A secondary level of engagement occurs through Bible studies involving similar texts with men in general and men who would use the Bible to justify their abusive behavior in particular. However, they must be Bible studies that can tolerate ambiguity. Unfortunately, this becomes problematic with so many who want to use the Bible and the contemporary Bible study as a means of controlling behavior, particularly with groups of abusive men. Finally, the heart of the matter is whether we regard the Bible as prescriptive or transformative. It is to risk asking the question to and with others–what does it do to us to read the story of David and Bathsheba from Bathsheba's perspective? What does it mean to consider a women as an equal child of God who should not be coerced by my violence? Such discussions can help men to challenge their personal metaphors and become nonviolent and respectful toward all women.

NOTES

1. Al Miles, *Domestic Violence: What Every Pastor Needs to Know*. Minneapolis: Fortress Press, 2000, 19.

2. Phy, Allene Stuart, Editor, *The Bible and Popular Culture in America*. Philadelphia: Fortress Press, 1985, 22.

3. Gomes, Peter. *The Good Book: Reading the Bible With Mind and Heart*. New York: Avon Books, 1996, xiii.

4. In particular, Judges 19:1-30, which appears as chapter 3, "An Unnamed Woman: The Extravagance of Violence," in Phyllis Trible, *Texts of Terror: Literary-Feminist Readings of Biblical Narratives* (Philadelphia: Fortress Press, 1984), 65-91 passim.

5. Meyer, "A Lack of Laments in the Church's use of the Psalter," 1993, 73ff.

6. Brueggeman, Walter. *The Message of the Psalms: A Theological Commentary, Augsburg Old Testament Studies*. Minneapolis: Augsburg, 1984, 53.

7. Brueggeman, Walter. "The Formfulness of Grief." *Interpretation*, 1977, 265.

8. Gomes, 58.

9. Wilmore, Gayraud. *Black Religion and Black Radicalism: An Interpretation of the Religious History of Afro-American People*. Second Edition, Revised and Enlarged. Maryknoll: Orbis Books, 1983, 9.

10. Grant, Jacquelyn. *White Women's Christ and Black Women's Jesus: Feminist Christology and Womanist Response*. Atlanta: Scholars Press, 1989, 203-230.

11. Wilmore and Cone, 1979, 421.

12. Kvam, Kristen, Linda S. Schearing, and Valaries H. Ziegler, Editors, *Eve & Adam: Jewish, Christian, and Muslim Readings on Genesis and Gender*. Bloomington, Indiana: Indiana University Press, 1999, 8.

13. Pittman III, Frank. *Turning Points: Treating Families in Transition and Crisis*. New York: W.W. Norton & Company, 1987, 287.

14. Kvam et al, 387.

15. Niebuhr, H. Richard. *Christ and Culture*. New York: Harper & Brothers, 1951, 188.

16. Niebuhr, 146.

17. Susan T. Foh, Woman and the Word of God: A Response to Biblical Feminism, 394.

18. Kvam et al., 387.

19. Weems, Renita. *Battered Love: Marriage, Sex, and Violence in the Hebrew Prophets*. Minneapolis: Augsburg Fortress, 1995, 31f.

20. Ibid. 34.

21. Hossick, Jeffrey. "An Understanding of a Contribution of Metaphor and Music in the Healing of the Isolation Dynamic of Shame." Ph.D. diss., Minneapolis: Luther Seminary, 2002, 21f.

22. Ibid., 16.

23. Ibid., 59.

24. Ibid., 75.

25. Ibid., 151f.
26. Paul Ricoeur, "Philosophical and Biblical Hermeneutics" *From Test to Action*, James M. Edie, ed. (Evanston: Northwestern University, 19), 100. Paul Ricoeur, "Critique of Religion," *The Philosophy of Paul Ricoeur: An Anthology of His Work*, ed. Charles Reagan and David Stewart (Boston: Beacon Press, 1978), 219.
27. Hossick, 161.
28. The Interpreter's Bible, Volume 2, 2 Samuel 11, 1990, 1098.
29. Datcher, Michael. *Raising Fences: A Black Man's Love Story*. New York: Riverhead Books, 2001, 257f.
30. Gomes, 349.

WORKS CITED

Brueggeman, Walter. "The Formfulness of Grief." *Interpretation*, 1977, 31.

Brueggeman, Walter. *The Message of the Psalms: A Theological Commentary, Augsburg Old Testament Studies*. Minneapolis: Augsburg, 1984.

Edie, James M. ed., Paul Ricoeur, "Philosophical and Biblical Hermeneutics" *From Test to Action* (Evanston: Northwestern University, 19), 100.

Gelles, Richard J. and Murray A. Straus. *Intimate Violence*. New York: Simon and Schuster, 1988.

Gomes, Peter. *The Good Book: Reading the Bible With Mind and Heart*. New York: Avon Books, 1996.

Grant, Jacquelyn. "Black Theology and The Black Woman." in *Black Theology: A Documentary History, 1966-1979*. Gayraud Wilmore and James Cone, Editors. Maryknoll: Orbis Books, 1979.

Grant, Jacquelyn. *White Women's Christ and Black Women's Jesus: Feminist Christology and Womanist Response*. Atlanta: Scholars Press, 1989.

Hossick, Jeffrey. "An Understanding of a Contribution of Metaphor and Music in the Healing of the Isolation Dynamic of Shame." PhD diss., Minneapolis: Luther Seminary, 2002.

Kvam, Kristen, Linda S. Schearing, and Valaries H. Ziegler, Editors, *Eve & Adam: Jewish, Christian, and Muslim Readings on Genesis and Gender*. Bloomington, Indiana: Indiana University Press, 1999.

Miles, Al. *Domestic Violence: What Every Pastor Needs to Know*. Minneapolis: Fortress Press, 2000.

Niebuhr, H. Richard. *Christ and Culture*. New York: Harper & Brothers, 1951.

Pittman III, Frank. *Turning Points: Treating Families in Transition and Crisis*. New York: W.W. Norton & Company, 1987.

Phy, Allene Stuart, Editor, *The Bible and Popular Culture in America*. Philadelphia: Fortress Press, 1985.

Reagan, Charles, and David Stewart, editors, "Paul Ricoeur, "Critique of Religion," *The Philosophy of Paul Ricoeur: An Anthology of His Work*, ed. (Boston: Beacon Press, 1978), 219.

Trible, Phyllis. *Texts of Terror: Literary-Feminist Readings of Biblical Narratives.* Philadelphia: Fortress Press, 1984.

Weems, Renita. *Battered Love: Marriage, Sex, and Violence in the Hebrew Prophets.* Minneapolis: Augsburg Fortress, 1995.

Wilmore, Gayraud. *Black Religion and Black Radicalism: An Interpretation of the Religious History of Afro-American People.* Second Edition, Revised and Enlarged. Maryknoll: Orbis Books, 1983.

Men Helping Men to Become Pro-Feminist

James Newton Poling
with Christopher Grundy and Hahnshik Min

SUMMARY. In this article, Poling explores the process of mentoring and mutual accountability between men who struggle to be pro-feminist and nonviolent. Two students share their own struggles with changing awareness and their responsibility to prevent violence against women. They focus on issues of worship in local congregations where there are men who have been violent. Poling responds with an analysis of the stages of conversion for pro-feminist men. *[Article copies available for a fee from The Haworth Document Delivery Service: 1-800-HAWORTH. E-mail address: <docdelivery@haworthpress.com> Website: <http://www.HaworthPress.com> © 2002 by The Haworth Press, Inc. All rights reserved.]*

KEYWORDS. Sexual and domestic violence, male identity, religion, worship

Men are not naturally pro-feminist; we enjoy our power and privileges; we have to be converted to a new way of thinking and acting.[1] My own conversion[2] started in 1985 when I worked with a feminist-oriented mental health agency that focused on incest. My dramatic experience of seeing male violence in this setting challenged my thinking on

---

[Haworth co-indexing entry note]: "Men Helping Men to Become Pro-Feminist." Poling, James Newton with Christopher Grundy, and Hahnshik Min. Co-published simultaneously in *Journal of Religion & Abuse* (The Haworth Pastoral Press, an imprint of The Haworth Press, Inc.) Vol. 4, No. 3, 2002, pp. 107-122; and: *Men's Work in Preventing Violence Against Women* (ed: James Newton Poling, and Christie Cozad Neuger) The Haworth Pastoral Practice Press, an imprint of The Haworth Press, Inc., 2002, pp. 107-122. Single or multiple copies of this article are available for a fee from The Haworth Document Delivery Service [1-800-HAWORTH, 9:00 a.m. - 5:00 p.m. (EST). E-mail address: docdelivery@haworthpress.com].

many levels and initiated a process of reconsidering my personal and professional identity. With the help of many colleagues and friends, I have continued to change over the years since and tried to be faithful to a pro-feminist vision.

Since my conversion began, I have accompanied other men in the process of change. Over the years a few have stood out because they have taken the pro-feminist theories more seriously than others. This article is a reflection with two such men on the impetus and process of change. Christopher Grundy and Hahnshik Min are two recent students who have made a serious attempt to understand the issues of solidarity of men with women so that male violence against women can be prevented. In recent classes on issues of power and abuse, they decided to write papers about theology and worship in which they revealed aspects of their own transformation. I have drawn on the papers they shared with me and then added reflections from my experience. They have read and given approval for this article.

CHRISTOPHER GRUNDY [3]

Christopher began his paper by reflecting on the experiences that initiated his own process of conversion and brought him to my classes.

"In one sense I have never worshipped alongside a man I knew to be an abuser. That is, in my years growing up in the church, and in eight years of pastoral ministry, I have never known a man who admitted committing violence against women or children. Likewise, no one in the churches I have attended or served has ever disclosed the fact of their abuse by someone I knew. Nor have I ever participated in worship in a context where male abusers have been together as an identified group, in a context of therapy or incarceration."

"In another sense, however, I have become increasingly aware of the fact that when I participate in worship, I am invariably worshipping with abusers. . . . If I have not been aware of abusers in my worship experience, it is perhaps more than anything else a critique of my own ignorance, my failure as a pastor to help create an environment where abuse could be disclosed, and my lack of self-awareness as an agent of male violence."

"The personal experiences that have led me to study the topic of worship and male violence have come primarily through dating relationships. Throughout my educational years, from high school through seminary, I was increasingly overwhelmed by the prevalence of male violence as reported by the women that I dated. Before I ever learned the statistics, I heard story after personal story of childhood sexual abuse, date rape, and ongoing battery. My senior year in college a woman I was dating was the victim of an attempted rape. She had left her dorm room unlocked thinking that I might stop by."

"I was angry and self-righteous about all of this violence, but it was not until late in my seminary years, reading John Stoltenberg's *Refusing to Be a Man*,[4] that I was able to move beyond anger, self-righteousness, and a kind of blanket 'gender guilt' to personal critical reflection. As I entered the parish and began leading worship, I also began to come to terms with my own coercive and abusive behaviors as an "ordinary" socialized male. Reflection on my own behaviors, reflection on the social construction of masculinity, and my work as a leader of worship have led me toward an interest in worship, and particularly sacramental worship, that is not complicit in the male abuse of power."

Later, Christopher reflected on the influences, both literary and experiential, that continued to shape his process of his conversion while he participated in classes with me.

"An important source of learning was from Dr. Poling's article, 'Male Violence Against Women and Children.'[5] The article contrasted the 'traditional liberal' view of violence against women and children, which focuses on individual pathologies and education, with a feminist/womanist approach that pays more attention to social realities. This contrast reinforced for me the fact that male violence cannot be unlearned through the education of individuals or even small groups. If male violence occurs not simply due to a given man's blind compliance with social forces, but occurs in order to maintain both personal and societal male dominance and control, then simply raising the awareness of particular individuals will make little headway in the face of an overwhelming cultural force. Especially in the lives of men who are actively abusive the competition between ideologies and patterns of behavior will be hopelessly one-sided."

"Another important learning experience took place during my interview with the director of a local shelter for battered women. She was clearly proud of the process of professionalization that had taken place at their shelter in the last couple of decades. She was clear, however, that progress had been made, both locally and nationally, primarily due to the political women's movement of the 1960s and the national shelter movement of the 1980s. She credited these political movements with pushing her agency to begin sheltering abused women in the first place."

"A third significant learning experience was the video 'Macho'[6] that we watched in class. Seeing an actual group of Nicaraguan men working to advocate for change in their society, both on a personal and social level, gave me a picture of what might be possible, for example, in my denomination. It also helped me to see even more clearly the connections between national and cultural dynamics and the lives of women and men in local communities. Any liturgical approach to male abusers in the congregational context must be undertaken in conjunction with and in order to reinforce other forms of peer influence, including participation in social and political movements of men resisting violence. In isolation, liturgical efforts will be as ineffective as individual therapeutic efforts have been."

Using the insights he had gained, Christopher then went on to reflect critically upon weekly worship.

"Central to any liturgical practice must be the priority of the experience of women who are survivors of male violence. Men have a tendency to change the focus to their own experience and ignore the experiences of women. Because abusers lack empathy or understanding of their victims, a persistent focus on the experience and needs of women as survivors in worship serves one of the needs of abusers as well; the need to be confronted with the experience of those they harm."

"Also related is one of the most important methodological insights I gained this term. In *The Abuse of Power*,[7] Dr. Poling emphasized the importance of accountability, saying, 'I have slowly come to see that others have insights that are crucial to my own life and well-being. I have been in dialogue with those who can correct my distortions and help me say what needs to be said.' Not only was this a new and important insight for me in my own academic work, but it has profound implications for worship as well. When have male pastors ever considered practical ways in which their design and leadership of worship could be made accountable to women?"

"Lastly, my ideas about God's forgiveness and the Christian community's forgiveness have changed significantly. In recent years, while working as an associate pastor, I was always uncomfortable when the senior pastor would pronounce in the name of Jesus that our sins were forgiven. I now believe that forgiveness should be seen as one aspect of a process that tries to place priority on right relationship and reconciliation where possible. God's grace which helps us on the road to right relationship may not be the same as God's forgiveness."

"Combined, these insights lead to the following conclusion: Congregational worship that hopes to address the needs of abusers must make intentional efforts to keep the experience of women, especially as survivors, as well as the safety of women, prominent in the worship of the congregation. Such worship must also include mechanisms for ongoing accountability to women. Congregational worship that hopes to address issues of male violence must not simply make reference to, but somehow engage in a process that holds men accountable, and helps them to work toward right relationship more than forgiveness."

HAHNSHIK MIN [8]

"Do the perpetrators of male violence deserve to worship God? Are they worthy of God's love? These questions have haunted me since I have been studying the issue of male violence against women and children. My encounter with the topic of male violence through books and articles has encouraged me to look at myself honestly and find my own tendency to be violent and abusive in my personal relationships. My study also forced me to examine critically the male-centered religion and culture that makes male violence easily happen."

"I do not have any professional relationships with abusers as a pastor. It is very likely, however, that I have met them in my life as the fathers of my friends, cousins, and children that I teach at church. The lack of firsthand experience with the perpetrators is the limitation of my thinking about worship with abusers. Even with this limitation, I hope to find God's healing presence in perpetrators and in myself as we work to be nonviolent toward women partners. Another hope for this project is to make myself ready to deal with the issue of male violence in my future ministry."

"Based on my research, I must assume that significant numbers of survivors and perpetrators are worshipping in the congregation where I am serving now and will serve in the future even though I do not know who most of them are. What is the proper pastoral response to this reality of male violence? How do I engage in planning and worship leadership with this newly acquired knowledge? Based on readings and personal observation, it is not unfair to say that the church has done little more than keep silent and blame the victims. Most church leaders have treated the topic of male violence as a taboo, unwilling to admit that it is happening in the church. Many of our church leaders have tended to believe stories from men and have ignored the voices of women, which has led to blaming women for being seductive."

"In consultation with James Poling, I have developed three principles for a healing service for perpetrators. First, the voice of victims/survivors must be present and predominant in the worship atmosphere. The service must intentionally give power to the voice of victims/survivors so that they can serve as the context of accountability for their abusers. An immediate problem is that the church is not safe enough for survivors to be open and forthright about their experiences. Rather, they tend to be misunderstood, blamed for their own experience of abuse, and marginalized as emotionally unstable. The church must critically examine its treatment of victims/survivors and change the attitudes and behaviors that marginalize them instead of abusers. In worship services on domestic violence the voices of survivors are given presence through their stories, songs, prayers, and poems. Such a process of planning requires an interdisciplinary team of feminist pastors and therapists who are committed to the domestic violence movement and know the literature so they can make the important decisions about what is appropriate for such a service."

"Second, the ritual of confession and forgiveness of sins needs to be conditional. The worship must focus on the eschatological dimension, rather than present a completed declaration of healing and forgiveness. For example, the words, 'you are forgiven' found in many traditional liturgies must not be used because it ignores the fact that forgiveness for abusers is a process of healing and accountability over time. Because of the church's notorious misuse of cheap forgiveness, it is important to emphasize the need for continued repentance for abusers and a commitment to be nonviolent. Fortunately, there are many biblical verses that emphasize the conditional nature of forgiveness. For example, Mark 17:3, 'If another disciple sins, you must rebuke the offender, and *if there is repentance*, you must forgive."

"The third principle is the accountability of male worship leaders. The healing worship cannot be done only by males without input from the victims/survivors and their advocates. Before and after the actual worship, male leaders have to be open to correction from the standpoint of victims/survivors. This can be done through feedback sessions from female pastors and therapists who work regular with victims/survivors. Organizing such accountability structures for worship leaders is one of the challenges of planning such a service since most male pastors are accustomed to being in charge without accountability to those who are marginalized."

JIM POLING'S REFLECTIONS

Christopher and Hahnshik were well on their way to pro-feminist thinking and acting before I met them. Even though they both grew up in the typical patriarchal culture where male dominance was taken for granted and violence against women was unseen and unspoken, they were troubled by some of the things they saw. Christopher had female friends who talked about their experiences of violence from men. And he listened. The women had been empowered by the feminist movement and the public debates about violence against women to speak about their own personal experiences. The women were willing to trust him with their personal experiences. Christopher and Hahnshik believed the stories they heard from women, even though they lacked an adequate theory and theology for understanding. Hahnshik was trained as a social worker before seminary and learned to listen to women's experiences. In Korea he had not been confronted with issues of abuse, but when he started reading stories by women in his seminary classes, he was open to change. Both Christopher and Hahnshik were already open to pro-feminist ideas when I met them, even if they lacked a coherent theory to explain male violence.

One of the most serious deficits to their experience was the voice of the church. Hahnshik said, "Most church leaders have treated the topic of male violence as a taboo, unwilling to admit that it is happening in the church." Christopher said: "I have never known a man who admitted committing violence against women or children. Likewise, no one in the churches I have attended or served has ever disclosed the fact of their abuse by someone I knew." Their stories are typical of many men including me; I grew up in the 1950s and did not have any help to understand violence against women.

Christopher and Hahnshik were deeply affected by seminary classes that required regular reading about theories of violence against women and field trips into the community where they had to confront violence against women. I feel gratified that my writing has helped to provide roadmaps through some of the difficult issues such as forgiveness and accountability. Although no book by itself can lead to conversion unless the person is ready to hear and is open to change but reading is important. Frank Pittman, the famous family therapist, says that he was confronted by Betty Carter, another famous family therapist, in 1984. "I said something insensitive at a workshop. My host took me to Betty Carter to be enlightened, which was great. She gave me a list of books to read, telling me that I shouldn't speak in public until I read 30 books on feminism. So I did, and was very much enlightened."[9] The theoretical re-orientation that comes from reading feminist writers is crucial for conversion of men to a pro-feminist position.

Another insight is that conversion requires examination of one's personal attitudes and behaviors. Christopher says he became aware of his ignorance and his "lack of self-awareness as an agent of male violence." Hahnshik says that "I was forced to look at myself honestly and find my own tendency to be violent and abusive in my personal relationships." This personal dimension is emphasized by most feminist writers and by the pro-feminist men's activist groups.[10] Until a man examines his own participation in male violence, he cannot experience conversion to a pro-feminist position. All men have internalized an acceptance of male dominance from their families and the institutions of society. Many men have an investment in being good men who are innocent of any violence. Religious men who want to be seen as righteous and trustworthy often have an especially difficult time dealing with their own complicity and abusive behaviors. Confession and exploring these attitudes and behaviors is a crucial part of the conversion process.

Through their study, Christopher and Hahnshik became disenchanted with and critical of the patriarchal theories they had inherited and looked for more adequate theories. Hahnshik said: "Many of our church leaders have tended to believe stories from men and have ignored the voices of women, which has led to blaming women for being seductive." Patriarchy often confuses violence and sexuality by saying that men are forced to be violent by the seductive actions of women. Christopher said: "It was not until late in my seminary years, reading John Stoltenberg's *Refusing to Be a Man*, that I was able to move beyond anger, self-righteousness, and a kind of blanket "gender guilt" to personal critical reflection." Beginning to see through the lies of patriarchy is an important developmental step in the conversion process. Kathleen Carlin, founding director of Men Stopping Violence, puts it this way:

> I'm not sure why I was surprised at the intense resistance to putting victims' safety first. I know that to put women's interests ahead of men's so fundamentally violates the status quo that we all react with terror and confusion at the thought. Women know that to put women's interests ahead of men's makes women a more prominent target for men's rage. We, as women, feel safer with what Martin Dufresne calls the "trickle down" model for ending violence: We would prefer to treat the symptoms of that violence

and hope for the best than to call attention to the deeply embedded ideology of male supremacy that sanctions it.[11]

Christopher and Hahnshik agree on several important aspects of the conversion process: (1) listening to women's stories of violence, (2) accountability of men to women who are survivors of violence and their advocates, (3) the importance of social analysis of the roots of patriarchy and violence against women and activism in the political movements to prevent such violence, and (4) theological reflection on the beliefs and practices of churches that contribute to male violence against women.

Listening to women's stories is a key factor influencing many men to change their views. It is important for men to hear, believe, and provide support for women, even when the stories challenge their previous thinking. Christopher and Hahnshik came to understand that all worship and other ministries in the church must be planned in full knowledge of male violence against women, and that this commitment requires that women are involved as active agents. Women cannot be consigned by male leaders to passive roles where they are taken care of by men for their own good. Such a patronizing attitude is just a benevolent form of patriarchy. Even if women are involved in active planning of the church's ministries, patriarchy is still at work in the tendency of men to revert to dominance and women to be submissive to men. So pro-feminist pastoral leadership requires a constant effort to be in regular communication and solidarity work with women. Otherwise, the church engages in implicit forms of violence against women. According to feedback from feminist consultants, men tend to frequently overlook the extent to which women (even non-victims) are unwilling and unable to side with their own empowerment interests because it feels like they are jeopardizing their fragile safety. Women sometimes feel like other women are much more of a threat than men whom they feel they understand and know how to placate. Some women try to silence anything that will shift the status quo that they have learned to manipulate in relative safety. So men who engage in collaborative work with women have much to understand about the various strategies women use to survive in a patriarchal world. And women need to be supported, encouraged, and empowered by men as they work at their own pace to gain voice and strength to resist patriarchal arrangements.

Accountability. Christopher and Hahnshik both understand that even though they have adopted a pro-feminist position, they are still subject to the pressures of patriarchy from their previous socialization, the pressure of family and local community, the media with its sexualized and violent images, and from the 3,000 year history of patriarchal theology. This means that pro-feminist men are not trustworthy allies of women just because they have started a conversion process.

It can be hard for many male religious leaders to accept limited trust from women survivors and advocates. The church depends so much on trust that withholding it often feels like a betrayal. Many men personalize this issue and feel hurt if they are confronted on their latent sexism. The only cure for this problem is regular systems of accountability of men to women survivors and advocates. What has become a principle in many pro-feminist men's groups should be applied to all men in ministry. As men plan and carry out their ministries with men, women and families, they should regularly consult with women who have known the experience of violence and are capable of providing compassionate supervision of men who are trying to do the right thing. I made it a point to do this with my writing and never publish anything that is not reviewed by women who have the skills to give me feedback on whether my writing is safe for women. I seek out opportunities to co-teach with women as often as possible, and regularly communicate with a group of women about what I am doing in my everyday practices. When I had a pastoral psychotherapy practice with abusers, I had a women supervisor who had the authority to confront me with mistakes I was making.

Developing a supervisory relationship with women who can supervise on this level is not easy. If the relationship is too friendly, the full honesty required for accountability can be sabotaged. Often it is easier for a supervisor to go along than cause a conflict that makes the male supervisee uncomfortable. Thus it is possible for men to organize supervision that is ineffective and ceases to be a learning experience. On the other hand, if the relationship is too harsh, most men lose the ability to share deeply what they are thinking and feeling. Supervision becomes a test of wills and leads to emotional withdrawal. It is important to find a good balance of trust, support, and confrontation for a good supervisory relationship. But the difficulties of organizing good pastoral supervision should not be used as an excuse for moving away from the central purpose, namely, to prevent male violence and make church and society safer for all women.

Social Analysis and Political Action. Both Christopher and Hahnshik mention the importance of social analysis of gender power relationships and the need to take an explicit political position against male violence. The ability to do this requires a political feminist movement that works at both a theoretical and an activist level. At the theoretical level, it is crucial to have a theory of gender that adequately explains the prevalence of male violence against women. It is also necessary for such theorizing to be backed up by strong political activism that can respond to the backlash and attempts to reassert patriarchy. Judith Herman has one of the best descriptions of this issue in her book, Trauma and Recovery.

> The systematic study of psychological trauma depends on the support of a political movement. . . . The study of trauma in sexual and domestic life becomes legitimate only in the context that challenges the subordination of women and children. Advances in the field occur only when they are supported by a political movement powerful enough to legitimate an alliance between investigators and patients and to counteract the ordinary social processes of silencing and denial. In the absence of strong political movements for human rights, the active process of bearing witness inevitably gives way to the active process of forgetting. Repression, dissociation, and denial are phenomena of social as well as individual consciousness.[12]

There is a tendency among religious leaders to avoid conflict and explicit political positions, especially when it would cause division within the intimate community of the congregation. In order for a pastoral leader to speak and act courageously on the issues of male violence against women, it is crucial that he or she has support from a strong theoretical and political base. How can a pastoral leader respond to the many objections to defining family conflict as a problem of male violence? In reports from survivors, I have heard many ways the church blames women for male violence: "She is a very difficult woman; she never gave him a chance to be a man; she asked for it; she does not know her place; she doesn't understand anything except violence. She chose her bed and now she has to lie in it."

Responding to such misinterpretations requires a strong and well-integrated theory about gender power and the history of patriarchy, as well as a political base to which the pastoral leader can return for consultation and support. Several pastors who were former students called me after they tried to confront abusive parents and male abusers in congregations, only to be opposed by other pastoral staff and key lay leaders. In several cases, the pastor was identified as the problem and the violence he or she was trying to prevent was forgotten and ignored. The pastor turned to me, a former teacher who could understand and provide some support. But long-distance phone calls and email messages were not enough. I encouraged them to find a support group in their local communities. Agencies such as shelters for battered women, child abuse prevention programs or sexual assault prevention programs are good resources to connect with for ongoing supervision of pastoral care. The pastors needed an active political base to counteract the pressures they were under in the congregation. This is necessary for all of us who seek to do something concrete to prevent male violence.

Theological Reflection. Christopher and Hahnshik were aware of important theological issues involved in their conversion. In their papers, they both focus on the issue of how to handle the issues of forgiveness and reconciliation. Abusers and their advocates often demand forgiveness from survivors and the church to fulfill the command of the Bible to forgive. Given the central place of forgiveness in the official theologies of most churches, it is risky to raise questions about this doctrine. Even the Lord's prayer says, "forgive us our sins as we forgive those who sin against us." What would it mean to withhold forgiveness from a male abuser? Would it jeopardize the salvation of survivors because they are unable to forgive? Fortunately the Bible itself gives a more complex view of forgiveness and reconciliation than the official public liturgies of most churches. Alongside the command to forgive is the command to repent and be righteous. There are also many historical sources delineating the process of confession, repentance, and justification.[13] Preventing male violence confronts pastoral leaders with the need to rethink the relationship between repentance and forgiveness.

The problem of male violence necessitates our revisiting other similar theological issues. For example, God as omnipotent, omniscient, and perfectly loving is not a good model for male abusers because it too easily sanctions the patriarchal control and abuse by father-figures in family and church. Jesus as the loyal son who did not complain about the violence he experienced at the crucifixion is not a good model for victims/survivors who are caught in abusive families. We need to recover images of God and Jesus as angry, repentant, vulnerable, and collaborative. Fortunately there are many such images in the Hebrew Bible and the Christian New Testament.[14]

Such theological reformulations require great courage on the part of male religious leaders who convert to a pro-feminist understanding of gender power relations because new ideas challenge usual ways of thinking. Men who change begin to see how intertwined gender and theology are, and how changing one's understanding of gender raises fundamental questions about theologies inherited from the past. We need a strong feminist theology to help reformulate theological doctrines, and a strong feminist movement within the church to support those who are making the changes.

ACCOMPANIMENT

I have learned much from Christopher and Hahnshik and feel privileged to have accompanied them on part of their journey. Their courage to change has given me hope that male violence can be understood and prevented.

It is important for men to learn to accompany one another through conversion to pro-feminist thinking and acting. I believe the following is required for such accompaniment: (1) empathic support, (2) honest confession, (3) courageous confrontation, and (4) long-term commitments.

Empathic Support. Men are used to looking to women, not other men, for empathy in their emotional lives. Many men have male buddies to share activities but no male friends with whom they share their vulnerabilities. Converting to a pro-feminist way of thinking and acting is hard and requires support. To help with the struggle, men need to learn how to trust one another and believe that they will not be put down by competitive teasing and challenges or judged for being less than a man. Sharing vulnerability among men breaks one of the cardinal rules of patriarchy, namely, that men should be in control and should not show their weakness to another man. The most difficult feeling to share with another man is fear. As the categories of masculinity begin to crumble, all men become afraid. We realize how much our identity has depended on a reliable world of gender power relations. What will we become if we give up our attachment to such ideas and chart a new course? Few of us have models for this kind of change, and we need the understanding of other men to endure. We must learn how to have empathy for one another's pain as we try to change.

Honest Confession.[15] As men begin to have empathy with one another, we also have to learn how to be more honest about our fears of violence, and our own violent behaviors. At Men Stopping Violence, the pro-feminist activist group that has helped me with my growth, the workshops for men invariably ask a series of questions: *What is your earliest memory of violence? What did people around you say or do? What did you feel? What is your first memory of violence against women? Share a memory of time when someone put a woman down. What could a woman do or say that could cause you to become threat-*

ening or abusive? Have you ever hit or abused a woman or stopped her from doing something she wanted? What did people say or do? These questions force men to be honest about their own experiences with violence and abuse, especially attitudes and behaviors that have negative effects for women. Every time I participate in this exercise, I have a flood of memories that create shame and guilt because I have witnessed many acts of violence against women and inflicted emotional injuries on women I love. But speaking about these is taboo, especially with other men in an atmosphere of honest confession. It is okay to joke about such topics, to watch violence on TV, or to use such stories to trash women in general. But it is not typical for men to take responsibility for our own attitudes and behaviors in a vulnerable way. Men who want to change must learn to be comfortable with this level of honest confession and know how to support one another in the midst of the pain.

Compassionate Confrontation. In batterer's intervention programs, there is always a time when the batterers collude against the leaders by supporting one another's abusive behaviors. They become interested in the details of how one man abused his female partner, turning into a cheerleading group rather than a confrontational treatment group. The men revert to the traditional male behavior of bonding with one another at the expense of women. Such collusion is typical of patriarchy and must be confronted. However, most men only know how to confront in an abusive way, through put-downs and personal attacks. It is important to find the right balance so that confrontation clearly focuses in terms of what a man is sharing and yet is compassionate. In the midst of our sharing, we need other men who can say to us: *That was a terrible thing you did and you seem to feel awful about being abusive in that way. We have done similar things, and we will help you understand yourself better so you can be a different person.*

Long-Term Commitments. The changes we are seeking take a sustained commitment over a long time. Even as we are changing, we are bombarded by messages from family, church, and society that men must be powerful, controlling, invulnerable, and emotionally distant. We cannot escape these influences, and much of the time we are not aware of the thousands of ways they are present. This means that men must commit themselves to empathy, confession, and confrontation with other men over the long term. Men who are changing are subject to the same human temptations as all people: to withdraw from the struggle, to betray one another, to choose the easy way through, to give up when things get tough. Men's groups can be as dysfunctional as any other groups, and can do more damage than good. But we have to stay committed for a life-time to becoming the human beings God calls us to be.

CONCLUSION

In this article I have reflected, with the help of Christopher and Hahnshik, on the process of men's conversion to pro-feminist think-ing and acting. I have been inspired by the courage of these two men to think more carefully about this process and its various steps. They have helped me to continue examining my own life and make changes. We three have been through a dramatic process of change that moved from a lack of awareness of abusive behaviors, to a pe-riod of growing awareness because of the honest sharing of women about their experiences of violence, to belief in a set of principles that opened our eyes to a new way of being. We now try to listen to women's accounts of violence, hold ourselves accountable to women mentors and other men who are in the process of change, and continually examine the social realities and theology that inform our identities. Finally, we seek to accompany other men through the challenges of becoming pro-feminist for the sake of love and justice in the world. Because of this journey, our identities have been pro-foundly changed, yet we are in the process of still more change. We praise God for the grace to endure and understand more of the reality that God has in store for those who seek justice.

NOTES

1. Accountability: This article has been reviewed by the co-editor, Christie Neuger, to insure that it will not make church and society a more dangerous place for women.

2. Self-disclosure: I am 59 years old, married, Euro-American, a middle-class pro-fessional, a Presbyterian minister and professor of pastoral theology, care and counsel-ing at Garrett-Evangelical Theological Seminary, Evanston, Illinois, a United Methodist graduate and professional school.

3. Christopher Grundy is Euro-American, married, mid-thirties, an ordained United Church of Christ minister, a former pastor who is currently a PhD student in li-turgical studies at Garrett-Evangelical Theological Seminary. His paper is entitled: "Worshipping with Abusers: Insights from Power and Abuse."

4. John Stoltenberg, *Refusing To Be A Man: Essays on Sex and Justice.* New York, Penguin, 1990.

5. Poling, James N. and Christie. C. Neuger, *The Care of Men*. Nashville, TN, Abingdon Press. 1997. This article will soon be republished in *Understanding Male Violence*. St. Louis: Chalice Press, 2003.

6. "Macho," a video about AHCV, Asociacion de Hombres Contra La Violencia, Managua, Nicaragua and their visit to San Francisco around 2000, sponsored by Family Violence Prevention Fund, 383 Rhode Island St., Suite 304, San Francisco, CA 94103. Information can be obtained from *Lucinda@cqm.co.uk* or Dean Peacock, (415) 252-8900 ext. 35.

7. *The Abuse of Power: A Theological Problem*. Nashville, TN, Abingdon Press. 1991, 18.

8. Hahnshik Min is a first generation Korean-American, married, early thirties, who is a licensed United Methodist pastor of Anglo and Korean congregations. His paper is entitled: "Beginning Thoughts on Rituals for Male Abusers." Used with permissoin of Chalice Press. J. Poling, Understanding Male Violence (2003)

9. "Frank Pittman Speaks," *Family Therapy Magazine,* special issue on Gender Perspectives, American Association for Marriage and Family Therapy, Vol. 1, No. 4, July-August, 2002, 13.

10. Men Stopping Violence is the pro-feminist activist and educational group that has most influenced me and which continues to provide national leadership for conversion of men. MSV, 1020 DeKalb Ave, # 25, Atlanta, GA 30307, 404-688-1376, *www.menstoppingviolence.org.*

11. Kathleen Carlin, in *Women Respond to the Men's Movement*, edited by Kay Leigh Hagan, San Francisco: Harper Collins, 1992.

12. Judith Herman, *Trauma and Recovery*. New York, N.Y., BasicBooks. 1992, 9.

13. David Livingston has explored the usefulness of the rigorous theology of confession and repentance according to St. Thomas Aquinas in *Healing Violent Men.* (Minneapolis: Fortress Press, 2001).

14. Many good articles about alternative constructive theology in light of male violence is available in Adams, C. J. and M. M. Fortune, *Violence Against Women and Children: A Christian Theological Sourcebook.* New York, Continuum, 1995.

15. Comment from Christopher Grundy: "In terms of the conversion process, I think that it was important for me to hear Dr. Poling break the code of silence and be as confessional as he was in his writing and, to a limited extent, in class. This opened a door for my own confessional thinking, and permitted me to break that code myself."

Index